EXTRA-ILLUSTRATED EDITION

∴

VOLUME 9
THE CHRONICLES
OF AMERICA SERIES
ALLEN JOHNSON
EDITOR

GERHARD R. LOMER
CHARLES W. JEFFERYS
ASSISTANT EDITORS

COLONIAL FOLKWAYS

A CHRONICLE OF
AMERICAN LIFE IN THE
REIGN OF THE GEORGES
BY CHARLES M. ANDREWS

NEW HAVEN: YALE UNIVERSITY PRESS
TORONTO: GLASGOW, BROOK & CO.
LONDON: HUMPHREY MILFORD
OXFORD UNIVERSITY PRESS

CONTENTS

ILLUSTRATIONS

ix

COLONIAL FOLKWAYS

∵

CHAPTER I

THE LAND AND THE PEOPLE

THE restless and courageous Englishmen who fared across the sea in the seventeenth century, facing danger and death in their search for free homes in the wilderness, little dreamed that out of their adventure and toil there would rise in time a great republic and a new order of human society. There was nothing to indicate that the settlements along the seaboard, occupying the narrow strip of land between the ocean and the mountain ranges, would eventually grow into a mighty union of states that would be called "the melting-pot of the world." The elements of that great amalgam of peoples, it is true, began to be gathered before the close of the colonial era; but the process of fusion made little progress during the years of dependence under the

1

British Crown. The settlements of the seventeenth century were widely scattered, separated by dense forests and broad rivers; and the colonists were busy with their task of overcoming the obstacles that confronted them in a primeval land. Even by the beginning of the eighteenth century there was little intercolonial communication to make the colonies acquainted with one another; and the thousands of immigrants, arriving yearly from the Old World and adding new varieties to the race types already present, rendered assimilation more difficult.

The entire colonial period was marked by shifting and unsettled conditions. The older colonies — Virginia, New England, Maryland, and New York — were undergoing changes in ideas and institutions. The Jerseys and the Carolinas were long under the control of absent and inefficient proprietors before they finally passed under the rule of the Crown. Pennsylvania, the last to be founded except Georgia, and the seat of a religious experiment in a City of Brotherly Love, was wrestling with the difficult task of combining high ideals with the ordinary frailties of human nature. In all these colonies the details of political organization and the available means of making a living were developed but slowly. England, too, the sovereign power across the sea, whose influence affected at every important point the course of colonial history, was late in defining and putting into practice her policy toward her American possessions. Not until after the turmoil of the war which ended with the Treaty of Utrecht (1713) do we begin to find a state of colonial society sufficiently at rest to admit of a satisfactory review. The half century from 1713 to 1763 is the period during which the life of the colonists attained its highest level of stability and regularity, and to this period, the training time of those who were to make the Revolution, we shall chiefly direct our attention. It will be an advantage, however, to preface a consideration of colonial life with a reference to the topography of the country and a review of the racial elements which made up its composite population.

The territory occupied by the colonists stretched along the American coast from Nova Scotia to Georgia. The earliest settlements lay near the ocean, but in some cases extended inland for considerable distances along the more important rivers. Behind this settled area, toward the foothills of the mountains, lay the back country, which after 1730 received immigrants in large numbers.

Except for settlements and outlying clearings, the colonial area, even near the sea, was densely covered with forests and contained to the end of this period many wild and desolate tracts of dismal swamp, drifting sand, and tangled jungle destined to remain for decades regions of mystery and fear, the resort of only fowl and beast, and the occasional refuge of criminals and outlaws. Gradually, as the years passed, the wilderness disappeared before the march of man, the wooded and rocky surface was transformed into fertile arable fields and pasture, the old settlements widened, and new settlements appeared. The number of colonists increased, and the pioneers steadily pushed back the frontier, setting up towns and laying out farms and plantations, rearing families, warring with the Indians and trading with them for furs, and turning to the best account the advantages that a bountiful though exacting nature furnished ready to their hand.

To the west of the colonists lay the boundless wilderness; on the east lay the equally vast ocean, the great highway of communication with the civilization of the Old World to which they still instinctively turned. If the land furnished homes and subsistence from agriculture, the sea, while also furnishing food, afforded opportunities for commerce and travel. Only by water, for the most part, could the colonists reach the markets to sell their fish, furs, and agricultural produce and to purchase those necessary articles of food, dress, and equipment which they could neither raise nor manufacture among themselves. Sometimes they trafficked in short voyages to neighboring colonies, and sometimes they sailed on longer voyages to England, the Continent, the Wine Islands, Africa, the West Indies, and the Spanish Main. Though the land and its staples often shaped the destiny of individual colonies, the most important single factor in bringing wealth and opportunity to the colonies as a whole was the sea. Those who journeyed upon the Atlantic thought as little of crossing the water as they did of traversing the land, and travelers took ship for England and the West Indies with less hesitation than they had in riding on horseback or in chaises over dangerous and lonely roads.

The colonial domain thus comprised regions which differed conspicuously from one another in climate, soil, and economic opportunity. But the races which came to dwell in these new lands were no less diverse than the country. At the close of the period here under review, that is, in 1763, the total white population of the region from Maine to Georgia was not far from 1,250,000. It is estimated that something more than a third of the inhabitants were newcomers, not of the stock of the original settlers. These newcomers were chiefly French, German, and Scotch-Irish. There were also in the colonies about 230,000 negroes, free and slave, 29,000 in the Middle Colonies, 16,000 in New England, and the remainder in the South. The influence of the non-English newcomers on colonial life was less than their numbers might suggest. The Scotch-Irish belonged rather to the back country than to the older settlements and — except in Pennsylvania, where they were something of a factor in politics — were not yet in the public arena. Their turn was to come later in the Revolution and in the westward movement. The same may be said of the Germans. Not many Germans in the colonies became as well known as John Peter Zenger, whose name is indissolubly associated with the liberty of the press in America. The Germans, however, as farmers contributed greatly to the prosperity of the communities where they cultivated their lands. Huguenots, Jews, and Highlanders remained in numbers near the coast and took part in the social, political, and commercial life of the older communities. The Huguenots and the Highlanders became influential planters, merchants, and holders of political office, men of enterprise and standing. The Jews on the other hand had no social or political privileges and made their mark principally in the field of commerce and trade.

Northernmost of the regions over which these many races were scattered lay New England, extending from the wilds of Maine through a beautiful rolling country of green fields and tree-clad slopes, to the rocky environs of the White Mountains, the Berkshires, and the Litchfield Hills. Here, according to the humor of a later day, the sheep's noses were sharpened for cropping the grass between the stones, and the corn was shot into the unyielding ground with a gun. Central and eastern New England was a region of low mountain ranges and fairly wide valleys, of many rivers and excellent harbors — a land admirably adapted to a system of intensive farming and husbandry. The variety of its staples was matched by the diversity of the occupations of its people. Fishing, agriculture, household manufactures, and trade kept the New Englander along the coast busy and made him shrewd, persistent, and progressive. He was unprogressive and slow in the more isolated towns and villages, where the routine of the farm absorbed the greater part of his time and attention.

In 1730 the New Englanders numbered, roughly, 275,000; in 1760, 425,000 or about a third of the entire white population of the thirteen colonies, and at the close of the Revolutionary War, 800,000. Somewhat less than half of these were under the jurisdiction of Massachusetts. Connecticut stood second in size and Rhode Island and New Hampshire were nearly equal. The New Englanders lived in compact communities along the coast and up the river valleys wherever land and opportunity offered, and in self-governing towns and cities, of which Boston, with about twenty thousand inhabitants, was by far the largest. [1]

The people of New England were mainly of English stock, with but a small mixture of foreign elements. The colony of Connecticut was the most homogeneous on the Atlantic seaboard. In parts of Massachusetts, New Hampshire, and Maine,

---

[1] Boston outrivaled in size every city in America except possibly Philadelphia, and as to which of the two was the larger is uncertain. Birket and Goelet, both writing in 1750, give diametrically opposite opinions on this point. Birket says that Philadelphia "appeared to be the largest city in our America," while Goelet calls Boston "the largest town upon the Continent."

hundreds of Scotch-Irish appeared between 1700 and 1750, some of whom eventually drifted down into Connecticut, where they formed a trifling and inconspicuous part of the population. These Scotch-Irish, who were not Irish at all except that they came from the north of Ireland, had much less influence in New England than in Pennsylvania, or in the back country of the South, where their numbers were five times as large as in the North and where their work as frontier pioneers was far more conspicuous. On the other hand, the Huguenots, fleeing from France after the revocation of the Edict of Nantes, in 1685, though never as numerous as the Scotch-Irish, nor ever as prominent as frontiersmen or founders of towns, had the gift of easy adaptation to the life of the older communities and remained in the urban centers, where they soon vied with the English as leaders in political and mercantile life. The names of Bowdoin, Cabot, Faneuil, Bernon, Oliver, and Revere add luster to the history of New England, while others of less note attained local success as artisans and tradesmen. The Jews, though their peers in business, were nowhere their serious rivals except in Newport. In this town, about the middle of the eighteenth century, Jews congregated. They came

either directly from Spain or from Portugal by way
of Brazil and the West Indies, and gave to that
growing Rhode Island seaport a distinctly commercial character. The only other foreigners in
New England were a number of Dutch, who were
not really "foreigners," as they came of the original settlers of New Netherland, having moved
eastward from the towns and manors along the
Hudson. Many negroes and mulattoes served as
farm hands and domestic servants, chiefly in or
near the seaports dealing with the South or with
the West Indies; and a few thousand Indians, more
often on reservations than in the households or
on the farms of the white men, survived in ever
dwindling remnants of their former tribes.

New York and Pennsylvania, though they were
closely akin to New England in climate and staple
products, bore little resemblance to that Puritan
world in the racial factors of their population or
the topographical features of their land.   New
England had a single dominant stock in a land of
many small communities and independent seaports.
New York and Pennsylvania, on the other hand,
with their satellite neighbors, the Jerseys and Delaware, contained a kaleidoscopic collection of people
of different bloods and religions.   Their life was

also less diversified and scattered, for it was closely associated with the marts of New York and Philadelphia. Each of these cities was situated on a superb body of water. The Hudson and the Delaware, like the Nile in Egypt, shaped to no inconsiderable extent the prosperity of the regions through which they flowed. But between these two cities there were noteworthy differences. New York was backward in colonial times, while Philadelphia, though less favorably situated, because the Delaware was a difficult stream for sailing vessels to navigate, leaped into commercial prominence within a decade of its foundation.

The differences between the provinces in which these cities lay is no less striking. Though possessing magnificent water facilities, the province of New York had as yet a very restricted territorial area, much of which was mountainous. Its broad interior, drained by the Hudson and Mohawk rivers, was of boundless promise for the future but of little immediate usefulness except as a source of furs and peltry, while the whole lay bottled up, as it were, and inaccessible to harbor and ocean, except through a narrow neck of land of which the island of Manhattan was the terminus. The people of the province — English, Dutch, and French, with a sprinkling of other nationalities — were much given to factional quarreling, and their political development was slow, for until 1691 they had no permanent popular assembly. Furthermore, the situation of the territory along the chief waterway from Canada of necessity exposed the province to constant French attack from the north and added to the distractions of politics the heavy burden of defense and the responsibility for peace with the Six Nations, whose alliance was so essential to English success. The population of the province nevertheless increased. In 1730 it was only 50,000; thirty years later it was more than 100,000; and, at the outbreak of the Revolution, 190,000. But in colonial times it always lacked cohesion and unity, owing to racial divisions and social distinctions and to its strangely shaped territory.

Philadelphia was the center of the far more compact colony of Pennsylvania and the seat of a more united, powerful, and dominant political party. The Quakers on principle avoided war and cultivated as far as possible the arts and advantages of peace. Though there was quarreling enough in the Legislature and a great deal of jockeying and rowdiness at elections, the stability and prosperity of the province were but little impaired. The city lay along the bank of a great river, in the midst of a wide, fertile agricultural country which included West Jersey and Delaware and which was inhabited by people of many races and many creeds, all tilling the soil and contributing to the prosperity of the merchant class. These merchants, with their dingy countinghouses and stores near the water-front had their correspondents all over the world, their ships in every available market. One of them, Robert Morris, boasted that he "owned more ships than any other man in America." Many of these merchants were possessed of large wealth and were the owners of fine country houses, as beautiful as any in the North, adorned with the best that the world could offer. The colonial mayors of Philadelphia, like those of London, were taken as a rule from the mercantile class.

The population of Pennsylvania increased from 50,000 in 1730 to more than 200,000 in 1763 — due in largest part to the thousands of Scotch-Irish and Germans who, from 1718 to 1750, poured into the colony. The bulk of the Scotch-Irish, urged westward by the proprietary government, which wanted to get rid of them, pushed rapidly into the region of the Susquehanna. The Germans usually settled in or near the old counties, where they could devote themselves to the cultivation of the soil and to the maintenance of their many peculiarities of life and faith, content to take little part in politics, though inclined to uphold the Quakers in their quarrels with the proprietors. Both the Scotch-Irish and the Germans moved onward as opportunity offered, journeying southwest through the uplands of Maryland and Virginia, west into the Juniata region, and northwest along the west branch of the Susquehanna, taking up lands and laying out farms. In this forward movement the Scotch-Irish were usually in advance, since their less developed instinct for thrift and permanence often led them to sell their holdings to the oncoming Germans and to trek to the edge and over the edge of the western frontier. The life of these Germans — Moravians, Mennonites, Schwenkfelders, Dunkards, and others — was marked by simplicity, docility, mystical faith, and rigid economy; that of the Scotch-Irish by adventure, conflict, and suffering. Before the land seekers of the southern tidewater had reached the back country, the Scotch-Irish and the Germans had entered the mountain valleys of Maryland, Virginia, and the Carolinas, and had developed a separate agricultural and industrial life of their own, independent of the tidewater but in close communication with the regions in the North whence they had come.

Beyond the southern boundary of Pennsylvania — famous later as Mason and Dixon's Line — lay two groups of colonies in a semitropical zone occupying the tidewater lowlands about the Chesapeake and the great rivers and sounds of the southern coast. These lowlands extended as far back as the "fall line," the head of river navigation, which curved from the present city of Washington through Fredericksburg, Richmond, and Fayetteville to Augusta. Within this area lay five colonies: Maryland, Virginia, the two Carolinas, and Georgia.

In 1760 the white population of the Southern Colonies was as follows: Maryland, 107,000; Virginia, 200,000; North Carolina, 135,000; South Carolina, 40,000; and Georgia, 6000. Of these colonies the last two had a proportion of blacks to whites vastly greater than the others. Although the Southern Colonies received at one time or another an accession of population from nearly every country of central and western Europe, they were in the main free from any large admixture of foreign stocks. Until after 1730 Maryland had few foreigners. At that time a few Germans crept down from Pennsylvania and others came in by way of the Virginia Capes, some of whom found lodgment in Baltimore and in 1758 erected a German church there. Virginia had at the beginning a few foreign artisans; later a number of Dutch and Germans, probably from New Amsterdam, occupied lands on the Eastern Shore; and at odd times Portuguese Jews from Brazil found refuge under its protection. But the only groups of foreigners in the colony were the Palatine Germans at Germanna, the French Huguenots at Manakintown, and a small body of poor but industrious Swiss at Mattapony. The dominant stock was English. On Albemarle Sound, in North Carolina, there were no foreigners, so far as can be ascertained. But after 1700 many Swiss and Palatine Germans toiled wearily overland from Virginia and founded New Bern; Huguenots settled on the Pamlico, German Moravians and Scotch-Irish poured into the back country; and Celtic Highlanders came up the Cape Fear and settled at Cross Creek (Fayetteville) and eventually became influential citizens of the colony.

South Carolina had a population which was a composite of English, Huguenots, and Germans.

WESTOVER, ON THE JAMES RIVER, VIRGINIA

A fine example of the Colonial architecture of the South. Built by William Byrd in 1749. Photograph by H. P. Cook, Richmond, Va.

The French element in the coast counties, however, numbered scarcely more than two per cent
of the whole, and the Germans — like the Swiss
in the same colony — were isolated and politi-
cally unimportant. Throughout the period the
center of the social and political life of South Carolina was at Charleston. Georgia had very few
foreigners, though she stood unique among her
sister colonies in possessing a small settlement
of Greeks and another of Salzburgers or Austrian
Germans.

Here and there among the colonies as a whole
were a few Italians, employed as gardeners, bota-
nists, or miniature painters; a few hundred Irish-
men, perhaps, though most of the Irish Celts began
their careers in America as indentured servants;
and once in a while a Czech or Bohemian, though
the identification is often doubtful. There were
Irish and Welsh Quakers in Pennsylvania, and a
few Danes are said to have come into New Hampshire with imported Danish cattle. Following the
Acadian Expulsion (1755), the French Neutrals or
Acadians were distributed among the cities from
Portsmouth to Savannah. These exiles presented
a pathetic picture of desolation and despair. They
were undesired, and were frequently charged with

2

crimes and misdemeanors by those who wished to get rid of them.

In time the colonists of the southern groups, with Virginians in the lead, pushed their settled area across the "fall line" and cut slowly and with great labor into the dense forests. Here they established farms and plantations and began the growing of wheat, a staple destined to become a dangerous competitor of the tobacco produced on lower levels. The upcountry was much healthier than the lowland and combined forest, pasture, and a wonderfully fertile arable soil with good water facilities and an equable climate. What had been in the seventeenth century but a camping ground for warriors, traders, and herders, became in the eighteenth century the seat of busy settlement and agriculture.

As the frontier was gradually pushed back by the movement of settlers from the coast, the newly won regions came under the control of the coast dwellers and reproduced much of the life of the older settlements. But such was not the case in Maryland nor in the far mountain valleys of Virginia and North Carolina. These regions did not receive their pioneers from the tidewater settlements. Central Maryland remained a wilderness until the Germans from Pennsylvania, carrying their goods in wagons and driving their cattle before them, entered the territory, took up tenancies under the land speculators of Annapolis, and began an era of small farms and diversified staples essentially different from the plantation life of the Chesapeake. As these pioneers passed on, they found homes along the Blue Ridge and in the Shenandoah and Yadkin valleys. And as the stream of homeseekers advanced southward, following the line of the mountains, farther and farther away from the coast and the older civilization, there arose a new community of American settlers living on small farms and tenancies and imbued with all the individualistic notions characteristic of the dweller on the frontier.

While the Virginians were clearing away the forests of their own back country and the Germans and Scotch-Irish, with the help of occasional pioneers from the coast, were filling the slopes and valleys of the lower Appalachian ranges with the hum and bustle of a frontier civilization, the old settlers of the Carolinas and Georgia remained little influenced by the call of the West. The old Albemarle settlement of North Carolina, founded by wanderers from Virginia in 1653, remained a comparatively poor and struggling community. It received but few additions by sea because of the sand-choked inlets and the fearful reputation of Cape Hatteras as a rendezvous with death for those brave enough to dare its storms and treacherous currents. On the other hand, these settlers ventured but short distances inland because of the no less terrible menace of the fighting Tuscarora Indians, who ranged over the region from seaboard to upland and carried terror to the hearts of even the boldest pioneers. Not until after the horrible massacre of 1711, from the effects of which the Albemarle settlement never fully recovered in colonial times, was an effort made to end the Tuscarora danger and to open up the lower and central part of the colony to occupation and settlement.

The assistance which South Carolina gave to her sister colony in revenging itself on the Tuscaroras brought to the knowledge of the leading men of Charleston the wonderful beauty and fertility of the land around the Cape Fear River and led to the founding of the second or southern settlement in North Carolina, first at Brunswick about 1725 and later at Wilmington, a town which eventually became the capital seat of the colony. But even the Cape Fear settlers, though laying out plantations

along the river and its branches, never passed
farther inland than the "fall line" at Cross Creek
(Fayetteville), the head of navigation on the river.
Throughout the period they remained more closely
in touch with their southern neighbors of South
Carolina than with those of the older region to
the northward and not only received from them
many accessions of numbers but also entered into
frequent intercourse of a social and commercial
nature. Though the Cape Fear planters raised
neither rice nor indigo, as did those of South Carolina and Georgia, they were similar to them in
manners, customs, and habits of life.

Just as the men of the Cape Fear region confined
their activities to the lower reaches of the river and
its tributaries, so the settlers to the southward —
at Georgetown, Charleston, and Savannah —
moved but short distances back from the coast
during the colonial period. At first there were only
a few plantations of South Carolina which lay as
much as seventy miles inland, and though after
1760 certain merchants of Charleston took up extensive grants of land on the upper waters of the
Savannah River, the only people in these colonies
who gave real evidence of the pioneer instinct were
the Germans. They entered South Carolina about

1735, pushed up the rivers into the region of Orangeburg and Amelia counties, and filled that frontier section with an industrious people who cultivated wheat, rye, and barley, entered into friendly relations with the Cherokee Indians, and lived in great harmony among themselves. As they increased in numbers and widened their area of occupation, some of them, by coming into touch with the Scotch-Irish who had pushed in from the north, eventually linked the back country civilization to that of the coast.

Such in broad perspective was the land of our colonial forefathers and such were the people who dwelt in it. The picture, when looked at more closely, has interesting features and a wealth of local color. Perhaps the most immediately striking, because one of the earliest and most fundamental, is the contrast between town and country.

CHAPTER II

THE tilling of the soil absorbed the energies of not less than nine-tenths of the colonial population. Even those who by occupation were sailors, fishermen, fur traders, or merchants often gave a part of their time to the cultivation of farms or plantations. Land hunger was the master passion which brought the men of the seventeenth and eighteenth centuries across the sea and lured them on to the frontier. Where hundreds sought for freedom of worship and release from political oppression, thousands saw in the great unoccupied lands of the New World a chance to make a living and to escape from their landlords at home. To obtain a freehold in America was, as Thomas Hutchinson once wrote of New England, the "ruling purpose" which sent colonial sons with their cattle and belongings to some distant frontier township, where they would thrust back the wilderness and create

23

a new community. Throughout the whole of the
colonial period this migration westward in quest
of land, whether overseas or through the wilderness, whether from New England or Old England
or the Continent, continued at an accelerating pace.
The Revolutionary troubles, of course, brought it
temporarily to a standstill.

In New England — outside of New Hampshire,
where the Allen family had a claim to the soil that
made the people of that colony a great deal of
trouble — every individual was his own proprietor,
the supreme and independent lord of the acres he
tilled. But elsewhere the ultimate title to the soil
lay in the hands of the King or of such great proprietors as the Baltimores and the Penns, to whom
grants had been made by the Crown. The colonist
who obtained land from King or proprietor was
expected to pay a small quitrent as a token of the
higher ownership. The quitrent was not a real
rent, proportionate to the actual value of the acres
held; it was never large in amount nor burdensome
to the settler; and it was rarely increased, whether
the price of land rose or fell. The colonists never
liked the quitrent, however, and in many instances
resolutely refused to pay it, so that it became in
time a cause of friction and a source of discontent

which played some part in arousing in America the desire for independence. Once when the people of North Carolina complained of the way their lands were doled out, the Governor replied that if they did not like the conditions they could give up their lands, which after all were the King's and not theirs. It was a small thing, this quitrent, but it touched men's daily lives a thousand times more often than did some of the larger grievances to which the Revolution has been ascribed.

The towns of New England were compact little communities, favorably situated by sea or river, and their inhabitants were given over in the main to the pursuit of agriculture. Even many of the seaports and fishing villages were occupied by a folk as familiar with the plow as with the warehouse, the wharf, or the fishing smack, and accustomed to supply their sloops and schooners with the produce of their own and their neighbors' acres. Life in the towns was one of incessant activity. The New Englander's house, with its barns, outbuildings, kitchen garden, and back lot, fronted the village street, while near at hand were the meetinghouse and schoolhouse, pillories, stocks, and signpost, all objects of constant interest and frequent concern. Beyond this clustered group of houses stretched the outlying arable land, meadows, pastures, and woodland, the scene of the villager's industry and the source of his livelihood. Thence came wheat and corn for his gristmill, hay and oats for his horses and cattle, timber for his sawmill, and wood for the huge fireplace which warmed his home. The lots of an individual owner would be scattered in several divisions, some near at hand, to be reached easily on foot, others two or more miles distant, involving a ride on horseback or by wagon. While most of the New Englanders preferred to live in neighborly fashion near together, some built their houses on a convenient hillside or fertile upland away from the center. Here they set up "quarters" or "corners" which were often destined to become in time little villages by themselves, each the seat of a cow pound, a chapel, and a school. Sometimes these little centers developed into separate ecclesiastical societies and even into independent towns; but frequently they remained legally a part of the original church and township, and the residents often journeyed many miles to take part in town meeting or to join in the social and religious life of the older community.

The New Englander who viewed for the first time the list of his allotments as entered in the

town book of land records had the novel sensation
of knowing that to all intents and purposes they
were his own property, subject of course to the law
of the colony, which he himself helped to make
through his representatives in the Assembly; subject, too, more remotely, to the authority of the
King across the sea. But the King did not often
bother him. He could do with his land much as he
pleased: sell it if need be, leave it to his children by
will, or add to it by purchase. The New Englander
loved a land sale as he loved a horse trade and any
dicker in prices; but he had a stubborn sense of
justice and a regard for the letter of the law which
often drove him to the courts in defense of his land
claims. Probably a majority of the cases which
came before the New England courts in colonial
times had to do with land. Yet there was little
accumulation of large properties or landed estates,
for such were contrary to the Puritan's ideas of
equality. Jonathan Belcher, later a Governor
of Massachusetts, had in eastern Connecticut a
manor called Mortlake, on which were a few un-
enterprising tenants, holding their land for a money
rental. There are other instances of lands let out
in a similar manner on limited leases, but the
number was not large, for, as Hutchinson said, the

Puritan's ruling passion was for a freehold and not a tenancy, and "where there is one farm in the hands of a tenant," he added, "there are fifty occupied by him who has the fee of it."

Outside New England there was greater variety of landholding and cultivation. The Puritan traveler journeying southward through the Middle Colonies must have seen many new and unfamiliar sights as he looked over the country through which he passed. He would have found himself entirely at home among the towns of Long Island, Westchester County, and northern New Jersey, and would have discovered much in the Dutch villages about New York and up the Hudson that reminded him of the closely grouped houses and small allotments of his native heath. But had he stopped to investigate such large estates as the Scarsdale, Pelham, Fordham, and Morrisania manors on his way to New York, or turned aside to inspect the great Philipse and Cortlandt manors along the lower Hudson, or the still greater Livingston, Claverack, and Rensselaer manors farther north, he would have seen wide acres under cultivation, with tenants and rent rolls and other aspects of a proprietary and aristocratic order. Had he made further inquiries or extended his observations to the west and north of the Hudson, he would have come upon grants of thousands of acres lavishly allotted by governors to favored individuals. He would then have realized that the division of land in New York, instead of being fairly equal as in New England, was grossly unequal. On the one hand were the petty acres of small farms surrounding the towns and villages; on the other were such great estates as Morrisania and Rensselaerwyck, where the farmers were not freeholders but tenants, and where the proprietors could ride for miles through arable land, meadow, and woodland, without crossing the boundaries of their own territory. If the traveler had been interested, as the average New England farmer was not, in the deeper problems of politics, he would have seen, in this combination of small holdings with large, one explanation, at least, of the differences in political and social life that existed between New England and New York.

What the traveler might have noticed in New York, he would have found repeated in a lesser degree in New Jersey and Pennsylvania. There, too, he would have seen large properties, such as the great tracts set apart for the proprietors and still awaiting sale and distribution, and such extensive estates as that of Lewis Morris, known as Tinton Manor, near Shrewsbury in East Jersey, and the proprietary manors of the Penns at Pennsbury on the Delaware and at Muncy on the Susquehanna. But there were also thousands of small fields belonging to the Puritan and Dutch settlers at Newark, Elizabeth, Middletown, Bergen, and other towns in northern New Jersey, and a constantly increasing number of somewhat larger farms in the hands of the Germans and Scotch-Irish in the back counties of Pennsylvania. The traveler would have noticed also, as he rode from Perth Amboy to Bordentown or Burlington, or from New Brunswick to Trenton, that central New Jersey was a flat, unoccupied country, with scarcely a mountain or even a hill in forty miles, that the sort of towns he was familiar with had entirely disappeared, and that along the highway to the Delaware and even from Trenton to Philadelphia, the country had only an occasional isolated farmstead. He would have met with no plantations in the southern sense of the word, with almost no tenancies like those at Rensselaerwyck, and with only a few compact settlements, such as the large towns of Trenton, Bordentown, Burlington,

Philadelphia, Germantown, and Lancaster, and the loosely grouped villages of the Germans, where the lands were held in blocks and the houses of the settlers were more scattered than among the Puritans. He would have learned also that, in Pennsylvania particularly, the needs of the proprietors, the demands of the colonists, and the character of the crops were leading to frequent sales and to the division of large estates into small and manageable farms.

What probably would have interested the New Englanders as much as anything else was the interdependence of city and country which was frequently manifested along the way. Unlike the Puritans, to whom countryseats and summer resorts were unknown and trips to mountain and seashore were strictly matters of necessity or business, the townfolk of the Middle Colonies residing in New York, Burlington, and Philadelphia had country residences, not mere cottages for makeshift housekeeping but substantial structures, often of brick, well furnished within and surrounded by grounds neatly kept and carefully cultivated. There were many stately "gentlemen's seats," belonging to the gentry of New York, between Kingsbridge and the city and on Long Island, for what is now Greater New York was then for the most part open country, hilly, rocky, and heavily wooded, interspersed here and there with houses, farms, fields, groves, and orchards of fruit trees, and threaded by roads, some good and some bad. Philip Van Cortlandt had his country place six miles, as he then reckoned it, from the city. Here at Bloomingdale, a village in a sparsely settled neighborhood — now the uptown shopping district of New York, somewhat north of the present public library — he was wont to send Mrs. Van Cortlandt and his "little family" to spend "the somer season." The Burlington merchants had their country houses near the Delaware on the high ground stretching along the river and back toward the interior. On the other hand, Philadelphia merchants, mayors, and provincial governors, whose city life was confined to half a dozen streets running parallel to the Delaware, had their country residences often twelve or fifteen miles away, sometimes in West Jersey, but more often in Pennsylvania itself, adjacent to the familiar and well-trodden highways. These roads, which radiated northwest and south from the river, formed arteries of supply for the markets and ships along the docks and, during certain times and seasons, afforded

THE PEABODY MANSION, DANVERS, MASS.

One of the best specimens of New England Colonial domestic architecture.   Built by "King" Hooper, of Marblehead, about 1754.

means of social intercourse between the business of the countinghouse in town and the pleasure of the dining hall and assembly room in the country.

To the Southerner, on the other hand, who passed observantly northward and viewed with discernment the country from Maryland to that "way down east" land of Maine which was as yet little more than a narrow fringe of rocky coast between the Piscataqua and the Kennebec, all these conditions of housing and cultivation must have seemed to a large extent strangely novel and unfamiliar. The Southerner was not used to small holdings and closely settled towns; his eye was accustomed to range over wide stretches of land filled with large estates and plantations. The clearings to which he was accustomed, though often little more than a third of the whole area, consisted of great fields of tobacco, grain, rice, and indigo, and presented an appearance essentially unlike that of the small and scattered lots and farms of the New England towns. He was unacquainted with the self-centered activity of those busy northern communities or the narrow range of petty duties and interests that filled the day of the Puritan farmer and tradesman. Were he a landed aristocrat of Anne Arundel or Talbot county in Maryland, he

3

would himself have possessed an enormous amount of property consisting of scattered tracts in all parts of the province, sometimes fifteen or thirty thousand acres in all. Many of these estates he was accustomed to speak of as manors, though the peculiar rights which distinguished a manor from any other tract of land early disappeared, and the manor in Maryland and Virginia, as elsewhere, meant merely a landed estate. But the name undoubtedly gave a certain distinction to the owner and probably served to hold the lands together in spite of the prevailing tendency in Maryland to break up the estates into small, convenient farms. Doughoregan Manor of the Carrolls with its ten thousand acres, for instance, remains undivided to this day.

By the wealthy Virginian the term manor was used much less frequently than it was in Maryland, while in the Carolinas and Georgia it was not used at all. In Virginia, even though the great plantation with its appendant farms and quarters in different counties could be reached often only after long and troublesome rides over bad roads through the woods, the estate was generally kept intact. Though land was frequently leased and overseers were usually employed to manage outlying properties, the habit of splitting up estates into small farms was much less common than it was in Maryland. Councilman Carter owned, we are told, some sixty thousand acres situated in nearly every county in Virginia, six hundred negroes, lands in the neighborhood of Williamsburg, an "elegant and spacious" house in the same city, stock in the Baltimore Iron Works, and several farms in Maryland. It was not at all uncommon for men in one town or colony to own land in another, for even in New England the owners of town lands were not always residents of the town in which the lands were situated.

It would be a mistake, however, to think of Maryland and Virginia as covered only by great plantations with swarms of slaves and lordly mansions. In both these Southern Colonies there were hundreds of small farmers possessing single grants of land upon which they had erected modest houses. Many of these farmers rented lands of the planter under limited leases and paid their rents in money, or probably more often in produce, labor, and money, as did the tenants of William Beverley of Beverley Manor on the Rappahannock. As many of the large estates in Maryland could not be worked by the owner, the practice arose of

renting some and of breaking up others for sale.
In this way there came into existence numbers of
middle-class landholders, who formed a distinctly
democratic element both in Maryland and Virginia.   They cultivated small plantations rang-
ing from 150 to 500 acres, not more than a third
of which was improved even by 1760.   Daniel Dulaney, the famous lawyer of Annapolis who had
made his money in tidewater enterprises, bought
land in central Maryland, which he rented out
to Germans from Pennsylvania and thus became a land promoter and town builder on an
extensive scale.

Though no such mania for land speculation
seized upon the Virginia planters, they were equally
zealous in acquiring properties for themselves beyond the "fall line" to the west, and some of
them endeavored to add to their wealth by pro-
moting the building of towns.   It was in 1745 that
Dulaney laid out the town of Frederick as a shrewd
business enterprise.   Eight years earlier, the second
William Byrd, one of the farseeing men of his time,
had advertised for sale in town lots his property
near the inspection houses at Shoccoe's.   This was
the beginning of Richmond, the capital of Virginia.
Less successful was Richard Randolph when, in

1739, he tried to attract purchasers to his town of Warwick, in Henrico County, modeled after Philadelphia, with a hundred lots at ten pistoles each, a common, and all conveniences for trade thrown into the bargain. But the only really important towns in these colonies during the colonial period were Annapolis and Williamsburg. In these towns many of the planters had houses which they occupied during the greater part of the year or at any rate when the Assembly was in session and life was gay and festive. Such other centers of population as Baltimore, Frederick, Hagerstown, Norfolk, Falmouth, Fredericksburg, and Winchester played little part in the life of the colonies except as business communities.

As the Albemarle region of North Carolina was settled from Virginia, the plantation and the tobacco field were introduced together, and along the sound and its rivers landed conditions arose similar in some respects to those in Virginia. The word "farm" was not used, but the term "plantation" was employed to include anything from the great estates of such men as Seth Sothell, one of the "true and absolute proprietors," and Philip Ludwell, Governor, to the small holdings of less important men, who received grants from the proprietors and later from the Crown in amounts not exceeding a square mile in extent. Though as a rule the holdings in Albemarle were smaller than elsewhere in the South and the conditions of life were simpler and less elaborate, the farmers were still freeholders, not tenants. The whole of this section remained less developed in education, religious organization, and wealth than other plantation colonies, and such towns as it had, Edenton, Bath, New Bern, and Halifax, were smaller and less conspicuous as social and business centers than were Annapolis, Williamsburg, and Charleston. Governor Johnston, who was largely responsible for the transfer of government from New Bern to the Cape Fear River, said in 1748: "We still continue vastly behind the rest of the British settlements both in our civil constitution and in making a proper use of a good soil and an excellent climate."

It was an important event in the history of North Carolina when Maurice and Roger Moore of South Carolina in 1725 selected a site on the south bank of the Cape Fear River, ten miles from its mouth, and laid out the town of Brunswick. With the transfer of the colony to the Crown in 1729, the settlement increased and prospered, lands were taken up on both sides of the river from its mouth to the upper branches, and plantations were established which equaled in size and productiveness all but the very largest in Maryland, Virginia, and South Carolina. At first many of the planters purchased lots in Brunswick, but afterwards transferred their allegiance to Wilmington on the removal to that town of the center of social and political life. No people in the Southern Colonies were more devoted than they to their plantation life or took greater pride in the beauty and wholesomeness of their country. They raised corn and provisions, bred stock — notably the famous black cattle of North Carolina — and made pitch, tar, and turpentine from their lightwood trees, and these, together with lumber, frames of houses, and shingles, they shipped to England and to the West Indies. The Highlanders who settled at Cross Creek at the head of navigation above Wilmington brought added energy and enterprise to the colony and developed its trade by shipping the products of the back country down the river and by taking in return the manufactures of England and the products of the West Indies. Some of them built at Cross Creek dwellings and warehouses, mills and stores, and set up plantations in the neighborhood; others, among whom were a few Lowland Scots, spread farther afield and bought lands even in the Albemarle region. To this section, after it had stagnated for thirty years, they brought new interests and prosperity by opening communication with Norfolk, in Virginia, as a port of entry and a market for their staples. They thus prepared the way for a promising agricultural and commercial development, which unfortunately was checked and for the moment ruined by the unhappy excesses and hostilities of the Revolutionary period.

South of Cape Fear lay Georgetown, Charleston, and Savannah, centers of plantation districts chiefly on the lower reaches of the rivers of South Carolina and Georgia. These plantations were characterized by a close union between town and country. South Carolina differed from the other colonies in that a considerable portion of her territory had been laid out in baronies under that clause of the Fundamental Constitutions which stipulated the number of acres to be set apart for colonists bearing titles of nobility. Thus it was provided that 48,000 acres should be the portion for a landgrave, 24,000 for a cacique, and 12,000 for a baron. Many colonists who bore these titles took up lands at various times and in varying amounts, but their properties, which probably never exceeded 12,000 acres in a single grant, differed in no way but name from any other large plantations. The most famous of the landgraves were Thomas Smith, who was Governor in 1695, and his son, the second landgrave, whose mansion of Yeomans Hall on the Cooper River, with all its hospitality, gayety, romance, and tragedy, has been graphically though somewhat fancifully pictured by Mrs. Elizabeth A. Poyas in *The Olden Time of Carolina.*

Most of the plantations of South Carolina and Georgia were smaller than those in Maryland and Virginia. A single tract rarely exceeded 2000 acres, and an entire property did not often include more than 5000 acres. These estates seem to have been on the whole more compact and less scattered than elsewhere. They lay contiguous to each other in many instances and formed large continuous areas of rice land, pine land, meadow, pasture, and swamp. Upon such plantations the colonists built substantial houses of brick and cypress, generally less elaborate than those in Virginia, particularly when they were described as of "the rustic order." There were also tanyards, distilleries, and soap-houses, as well as all facilities for raising rice, corn, and later indigo. At first the chief staple on these plantations was rice; but the introduction of indigo in 1745, with its requirement of vats, pumps, and reservoirs, and its plague of refuse and flies, though of great significance in restoring the prosperity of the province, gave rise to new and in some respects less agreeable conditions. The plantations were also supplied with a plentiful stock of cattle and the necessary household goods and furnishings. The following detailed description of William Dry's plantation on the Cooper River, two miles above Goose Creek, is worth quoting. The estate, which fronted the high road, is described as

having on it a good brick dwelling house, two brick store houses, a brick kitchen and washhouse, a brick necessary house, a barn with a large brick chimney, with several rice mills, mortars, etc., a winnowing house, an oven, a large stable and coach-house, a cooper's shop, a house built for a smith's shop; a garden on each side of the house, with posts, rails, and poles of the best stuff, all planed and painted and bricked underneath; a fish pond, well stored with perch, roach, pike, eels, and cat-fish; a handsome cedar horse-block or double pair of stairs; frames, planks, etc., ready to be fixed in and about a spring within three stones' throw of the house, intended for a cold bath and house over it; three large dam ponds, whose tanks with some small repairs will drown upwards of 100 acres of land, which being very plentifully stored with game all the winter season affords great diversion; an orchard of very good apple and peach trees, a corn house and poultry house that may with repairing serve some years longer, a small tenement with a brick chimney on the other side of the high road, fronting the dwelling house, and at least 400 acres of the land cleared, all except what is good pasture, and no part of the tract bad, the whole having a clay foundation and not deep, the great part of it fenced in, and upwards of a mile of it with a ditch seven feet wide and three and a half deep.

Most of the South Carolina planters had their town houses and divided their time between city and country. They lived in Charleston, Georgetown, Beaufort Town, and Dorchester, but of these Charleston was the Mecca toward which all eyes turned and in which all lived who had any social or political ambitions. Attempts were made in the eighteenth century, in this colony as elsewhere, to boom land sites for the erecting of towns on an artificial plan. In 1738, the second landgrave, Thomas Smith, tried to start a town on his Winyaw tract near Georgetown. He laid out a portion of the land along the bluff above the Winyaw River in lots, offered to sell some and to give away others, and planned to provide a church, a meetinghouse, and a school. But this venture failed; and even the more successful attempt to build up Willtown about the same time, although lots were sold and houses built and occupied, eventually came to nothing. The story of some of these dead towns of the South, whether promoted by natives or settled by foreigners, has been told only in part and forms an interesting chapter in colonial history.

In all the colonies, indeed, the eighteenth century saw a vast deal of land speculation. The merchants and shopkeepers in most of the large towns acted as agents and bought and sold on commission. Just as George Tilly, merchant and contractor of Boston, advertised good lots for sale in 1744, so John Laurens, Robert Hume, and Benjamin Whitaker in Charleston a little later were dealing in houses, tenements, and plantations as a side line to their regular business as saddlers and merchants. In the seventies the sale of land had become an end in itself, and one Jacob Valk advertised himself as a "Real and Personal Estate Dealer." The meaning of the change is clear. Desirable lands in the older settlements were no longer available except by purchase, and men were already looking beyond the "fall line" and the back country to the ungranted lands of the new frontier in the farther West.

CHAPTER III

COLONIAL HOUSES

It is well worth while for us at this point to look more in detail at the colonial towns to see the houses in which our ancestors dwelt and to note the architecture of their public edifices, for these men had a distinctive style of building as characteristic of their age as skyscrapers and apartment houses are of the present century. The household furnishings have also a charm of their own and in many cases, by their combination of utility and good taste, have provided models for the craftsmen of a later day. A brief survey of colonial houses, inside and out, will serve to give us a much clearer idea of the environment in which the people lived during the colonial era.

The materials used by the colonists for building were wood, brick, and more rarely stone. At first practically all houses were of wood, as was natural in a country where this material lay ready to every man's hand and where the means for making brick or cutting stone were not readily accessible. Clay, though early used for chimneys, was not substantial enough for housebuilding, and lime for mortar and plaster was not easy to obtain. Though limestone was discovered in New England in 1697, it was not known at all in the tidewater section of the South, where lime continued to the end of the era to be made from calcined oyster shells. The seventeenth century was the period of wooden houses, wooden churches, and wooden public buildings; it was the eighteenth century which saw the erection of brick buildings in America.

Up to the time of the Revolution bricks were brought from England and Holland, and are found entered in cargo lists as late as 1770, though they probably served often only as ballast. But most of the bricks used in colonial buildings were molded and burnt in America. There were brickkilns everywhere in the colonies from Portsmouth to Savannah. Indeed bricks were made, north and south, in large enough quantities to be exported yearly to the West Indies. As building stone scarcely existed in the South, all important buildings there were of brick, or in case greater strength were needed, as for Fort Johnston at the mouth of the Cape Fear River or the fortifications of Charleston, of tappy work, a mixture of concrete and shells. Brick walls were often built very thick; those of St. Philip's Church, Brunswick, still show three feet in depth. Chimneys were heavy, often in stacks, and windows as a rule were small. The bonding was English, Flemish, or "running," according to the taste of the builder, and many of the houses had stone trimming, which had to be brought from England, if it were of freestone as was suggested for King's Chapel, Boston, or of marble as in Governor Tryon's palace in New Bern.

Buildings of stone were not common and were confined chiefly to the North, where this material could be easily and cheaply obtained. As early as 1639 Henry Whitfield erected a house of stone at Guilford, Connecticut, to serve in part as a place of defense, and in other places, here and there, were to be found stone buildings used for various purposes. It has been said that King's Chapel, Boston, built in 1749–54, was the first building in America to be constructed of hewn stone, but this is not the case. Some of the early houses in New York as well as the two Anglican churches were of hewn stone. The Malbone country house near Newport, built before 1750, was also "of hewn stone and all the corners and sides of the windows painted to represent marble." There were many houses in the colonies painted to resemble stone, and some in which only the first story or the basement was of this material, while in many instances there were broad stone steps leading up to a house otherwise constructed of wood or brick. Stone for building purposes was therefore well known and frequently used.

Travelers who visited the leading towns in the period from 1750 to 1763 have left descriptions which help us to visualize the external features of these places. Portsmouth, the most northerly town of importance, had houses of both wood and brick, "large and exceeding neat," we are told, "generally 3 story high and well sashed and glazed with the best glass, the rooms well plastered and many wainscoted or hung with painted paper from England, the outside clapboarded very neatly." Salem was "a large town well built, many genteel large houses (which tho' of wood) are all pland and painted on the outside in imitation of hewn stone." By 1750 Boston had about three thousand houses and twenty thousand inhabitants; two-thirds of the houses were of wood, two or three stories high, mostly sashed, the remainder of brick,

A NEW ENGLAND PARLOR OF ABOUT 1800

Showing carved wooden mantel, combined table and fire screen, and spinet. In the Essex Institute, Salem, Mass.

Copyright 1907
by Lenz Furniture

substantially built and in excellent architectural taste.   The streets were well paved with stone, a thing rare in New England, but those in the North End were crooked, narrow, and disagreeable.   Worcester was "one of the best built and prettiest inland little towns" that Lord Adam Gordon had seen in America.   The houses in Newport, with one or two exceptions, were of wood, making "a good appearance and also as well furnished as in most places you will meet with, many of the rooms being hung with printed canvas and paper, which looks very neat, others are well wainscoted and painted."   New London with its one street a mile long by the river side and its houses built of wood, seemed in 1750 to be "new and neat." New Haven, which covered a great deal of ground, was laid out in nine squares around a green or market place, and contained many houses in wood, a few in brick or stone, a brick statehouse, a brick meetinghouse, and Yale College, which was being rebuilt in brick.   Middletown, though one of the most important commercial centers between New York and Boston and the third town in Connecticut, had only wooden houses.   Hartford, "a large, scattering town on a small river" (the Little River not the Connecticut is meant), was

4

built chiefly of wood, with here and there a brick dwelling house.

New York, with two or three thousand buildings and from sixteen to seventeen thousand people in 1760, was very irregular in plan, with streets which were crooked and exceedingly narrow but generally pretty well paved, thus adding "much to the decency and cleanness of the place and the advantage of carriage." Many of the houses were built in the old Dutch fashion, with their gables to the street, but others were more modern, "many of 'em spacious, genteel houses, some being 4 or 5 stories high, others not above two, of hewn stone, brick, and white Holland tiles, neat but not grand." A round cupola capping a square wooden church tower rising above a few clustering houses was all that marked the town of Brooklyn, while a ferry tavern and a few houses were all that foreshadowed the future greatness of Jersey City. Albany was as yet a town of dirty and crooked streets, with its houses badly built, chiefly of wood, and unattractive in appearance.

Southward across the river from New York were Elizabeth, New Brunswick, and Perth Amboy, the last with a few houses for the "quality folk," but "a mean village," albeit one of the capitals of the province of New Jersey. Burlington, the other capital, consisted "of one spacious large street that runs down to the river," with several cross streets, on which were a few "tolerable good buildings," with a courthouse which made "but a poor figure, considering its advantageous location." Trenton, or Trent Town, was described in 1749 as "a fine town and near to Delaware River, with fine stone buildings and a fine river and intervals medows, etc."

Philadelphia had 2100 houses in 1750 and 3600 in 1765, built almost entirely of brick, generally "three stories high and well sashed, so that the city must make (take it upon the whole) a very good figure." The Virginia ladies who visited the city were wont to complain of the small rooms and monotonous architecture, every house like every other. The streets were paved with flat footwalks on each side of the street and well illumined with lamps, which Boston does not appear to have had until 1773. Wilmington on the Delaware was a very young town in 1750, "all the houses being new and built of brick." Newcastle, the capital, was a poor town of little importance. There were but few towns in Maryland. Annapolis, the capital, was "charmingly situated on a peninsula, falling different ways to the water . . . built in an irregular form, the streets generally running diagonally and ending in the Town House, others on a house that was built for the Governor, but never was finished." This "Governor's House" afterwards became the main building of St. John's College. A majority of the residences were of brick, substantially built within brick walls enclosing gardens in true English fashion.

Across the Potomac was Williamsburg, the capital of Virginia and the seat of William and Mary College, built partly of brick and partly of wood, and resembling, it seemed to Lord Adam Gordon, a good country town in England. Norfolk, which was built chiefly of brick, was a mercantile center, with warehouses, ropewalks, wharves, and shipyards, while Fredericksburg, at the head of navigation on the Rappahannock, was constructed of wood and brick, its houses roofed with shingles painted to resemble slate. Winchester in the Shenandoah Valley was described in 1755 as "a town built of limestone and covered with slate with which the hills abound." It was the center of a settled farming country and its inhabitants enjoyed most of the necessities but few of the luxuries of life and had almost no books. It is described as being "inhabited by a spurious race of mortals

known by the appellation of Scotch-Irish." In all
of these towns were one or more churches, the
market house, prison, and pillory, and in the chief
city at the usual place of execution was the gallows
of the colony.

The older towns of North Carolina, Edenton,
Bath, Halifax, and New Bern, were all small, and
in 1760 were either stationary or declining. Their
houses were built of wood and, except for Tryon's
palace at New Bern — an extravagant structure,
considering the resources of the colony — the public
buildings were of no significance. Brunswick, too,
was declining and was but a poor town, "with a
few scattered houses on the edge of a wood,"
inhabited by merchants. Wilmington was now
rapidly advancing to the leading place in the province, because of its secure harbor, easy communication with the back country, accessibility to the
other parts of the colony, fresh water, and improved postal facilities. In 1760 it had about
eight hundred people; its houses, though not spacious, were in general very commodious and well
furnished. Peter du Bois wrote of Wilmington in
1757: "It has greatly the preference in my esteem
to New Bern . . . the regularity of its streets
is equal to that of Philadelphia and the buildings

are in general very good. Many of brick, two or three stories high with double piazzas, which make a good appearance."

Charleston, or Charles Town as the name was always written in colonial times, was the leading city of the South and is thus described by Pelatiah Webster, who visited it in 1765: "It contains ab^t 1000 houses with inhabitants 5000 whites and 20,000 blacks, has eight houses for religious worship . . . the streets run N. & S. & E. & W. intersecting each other at right angles, they are not paved, except the footways within the posts ab^t 6 feet wide, which are paved with brick in the principal streets." According to a South Carolina law all buildings had to be of brick, but the law was not observed and many houses were of cypress and yellow pine. Laurens said in 1756 that "none but the better class glaze their houses." The sanitary condition of all colonial towns was bad enough, but the grand jury presentments for Charleston and Savannah which constantly found fault with the condition of the streets, the sewers, and necessary houses, and the insufficient scavenging, leave the impression on the mind of the reader that these towns especially were afflicted with many offensive smells and odors. The total absence of any proper health precautions explains in part the terrible epidemics, chiefly of smallpox, which scourged the colonists in the eighteenth century.

Taking the colonial area through its entire length and breadth, we find individual houses of almost every description, from the superb mansions of the Carters in Virginia and of the Vassalls in Massachusetts to the small wooden frame buildings, forty by twenty feet or thereabouts, "with a shade on the backside and a porch on the front," and the simple houses of the country districts or the western frontier, hundreds of which were small, of one story, unpainted, covered with roughhewn or sawn flat boards, weather-stained, with few windows and no panes of glass, and without adornment or architectural taste. One traveler speaks of the small plantation houses in Maryland as "very bad, and ill contrived, there furniture mean, their cooks and housewifery worse if possible,"[1] and another says that an apartment to sleep in and another for domestic purposes, with a contiguous storehouse and conveniences for their live stock gratified the utmost ambition of the settlers in Frederick County.[2] Many a colonist north of the Potomac lived in nothing better than the "crib" or

[1] Birket, *Cursory Remarks*, 1750.   [2] Eddis, *Letters*, 1769–1777.

"block" house which was made of squared logs and roofed with clapboards. In contrast to the typical square-built houses of New England, the Dutch along the Hudson and even to the eastward in Litchfield County, Connecticut, built quaint, low structures which they frequently placed on a hillside in order to utilize the basement as living rooms for the family.

The better colonial houses were wainscoted and paneled or plastered and whitewashed, and the woodwork — trim, cornices, stair railings, and newel posts — was often elaborately carved. Floors were sometimes of double thickness and were laid so that "the seam or joint of the upper course shall fall upon the middle of the lower plank which prevents the air from coming thro' the floor in winter or the water falling down in summer when they wash their houses." Roofs were covered with tile, slate, shingles, and lead, though much of the last was removed for bullets at the time of the Revolution. Flat tiles, made in Philadelphia and elsewhere, were used for paving chimney hearths and for adorning mantels, and firebacks imported from England were widely introduced. Among the Pennsylvania Germans wood stoves were generally used, but soft coal brought as ballast from Newcastle,

Liverpool, and other ports in England and Scotland was also for sale. Stone coal or anthracite was familiar to Pennsylvania settlers as early as 1763, but until just before the Revolution was not burned as fuel except locally and on a small scale. Wood was consumed in enormous quantities and we are told that at Nomini Hall there were kept burning twenty-eight fires which required four loads of wood a day.[1]

There were few professional architects, for colonial planters and carpenters did their own planning and building. What is sometimes called the "carpenters' colonial style" was often designed on the spot or taken from Batty Langley's *Sure Guide*, the *Builders' Jewel*, or the *British Palladio*. Smibert, the painter and paint-shop man of Boston, designed Faneuil Hall and succeeded in creating a very unsuccessful building architecturally. The first professional architect in America was Peter Harrison, who drew the plans for King's Chapel, the Redwood Library, the Jewish Synagogue, and Brick Market at Newport, yet even he combined designing with other avocations. In truth there was no great need of architects in colonial days. Styles did not vary much, certainly not in New

[1] Fithian, *Diary*, 1767–1774.

England and the Middle Colonies, and a good carpenter and builder could do all that was needed. There were scores of houses in New England similar to Samuel Seabury's rectory at Hempstead, — a story and a half high in front, with a roof of a single pitch sloping down to one story in the rear, low ceilings everywhere, four rooms with a hall on the first floor, a kitchen behind, and three or four rooms on the second story.

The brick houses were more elaborate and were sometimes built with massive end chimneys, between which was a steep-pitched roof with dormers and a walk from chimney to chimney many feet wide. Other houses, made of wood as well as brick, had hipped roofs with end chimneys or roofs converging to a square center and a railed lookout. All the nearly 150 colonial houses still standing in Connecticut conform to a common type, though they differ greatly in the details of their paneling, mantels, cupboards, staircases, closed or open beamed ceilings, fireplaces, and the like. Some had slave quarters in the basement, others under the rafters in what was called in one instance "the Black Hole." Many of even the better houses were unpainted inside and out; many had paper, hung or tacked (afterwards pasted) on the walls; and in a few noteworthy cases in New England the chimney breasts were adorned with paintings. The floors were usually bare or covered with matting; rugs were used chiefly at the bedside, but carpets were rare.

Philadelphia, which was famous for the uniformity of its architecture, must have contained in 1760 many houses of the style of that built for Provost Smith of the College of Philadelphia. In addition to a garret this dwelling had three stories respectively eleven, ten, and nine feet high. The brick outside walls were fourteen inches thick and the partition walls, of the same material, nine inches. There were windows and window glass, heavy shutters, a plain cornice, cedar gutters and pipes. The woodwork, inside and out, was painted white, and all the rooms were plastered. No mention is made of white marble steps, but there may have been such, for no Philadelphia house was complete without them.

The Southern houses, both on the plantations and in the towns, varied so widely in their style of architecture that no single description will serve to characterize all. Such buildings as the Governor's palace at Williamsburg, Tryon's palace at New Bern, and the Government House at Annapolis were handsome buildings provided with conveniences for entertainment, and that at New Bern contained rooms for the gathering of assembly and council. The most representative Southern plantation house was of brick with wings, the kitchens on one side and the carriage house on the other, sometimes attached directly to the central mansion and sometimes entirely separate or connected only by a corridor. In the Carolinas and Georgia, however, there were many rectangular houses without wings, built of wood or brick, with rooms available for summer use in the basement. The roof was often capped with a cupola and commanded a wide prospect.

The dwelling houses of Charleston were among the most distinctive and quaint of all colonial structures. Some of them were divided into "tenements" quite unlike the tenements and flats of the present day, for, in addition to its independent portion of the house, each family had its own yard and garden. Overseers' houses were as a rule small, about twenty feet by twelve, with brick chimneys and plastered rooms. A typical Savannah house had two stories, with a handsome balcony in front and a piazza the whole length of the building in the rear, with a bedroom at one end and a storehouse at the other. The dining room was on the second floor, and everywhere, for convenience and comfort, were to be found closets and fireplaces. Among the gentry in a country where storms were frequent, electrical rods were in use, and in 1763 one Alexander Bell of Virginia advertised a machine for protecting houses from being struck by lightning, though what his contrivance was we do not know.

The town halls and courthouses generally followed English models, with public offices and assembly rooms on the upper floor and a market and shops below. The Southern courthouses were at first built of wood and later of brick, with shingled roofs, heavy planked floors, and occasionally a cupola or belfry. Those of the eighteenth century either included the prison and pillory or were connected with them. The inadequacy of jail accommodation was a cause of constant complaint. Not only did grand juries and newspapers point out the need of quarters so arranged that debtors, felons, and negroes should not be thrown together, but the occupants themselves protested against the nauseating smells and odors. In some of the prisons, it is true, a separate cage was provided for the negroes, and in North Carolina prison bounds, covering some six acres about the building, were laid out for the use of the prisoners, an arrangement which was not abolished till the nineteenth century.

In all the cities of the North and South stores and shops were to be found, occupying the first floor, while the family lived in the rooms above. As a rule, a shop meant a workshop where articles were made, a store a storehouse where goods were kept. But in practice usage varied, as "shop" was in common use in New England for any place where things were sold, and "store" was the usual term in Philadelphia and the South. An apprentice writing home to England in 1755 and trying to explain the use of the terms said: "Stores here [in Virginia] are much like shops in London, only with this difference, the shops sell but one kind or species of wares and stores all kinds." Some of these stores, particularly in Maryland and Virginia, were located away from the urban centers, in the interior near the courthouses at the crossroads, along the rivers at the tobacco inspection houses, or wherever else men congregated for business or public duty. They were often controlled by English or Scottish firms and managed by agents sent to America. They received their supplies from Great Britain and they sold, for credit, cash, or tobacco, almost everything that the neighborhood needed.

Varied as were the architectural features of colonial houses, they were paralleled by an equal diversity in the household effects with which these dwellings were equipped. It is impossible even to summarize the information given in the thousands of extant wills, inventories, and invoices which reveal the contents and furnishings of these houses. Chairs, bureaus, tables, bedsteads, buffets, cupboards, were in general use. They were made of hickory, pine, maple, cypress, oak, and even mahogany, which began to be used as early as 1730. From the meager dining room outfit of only one chair, a bench, and a table, all rough and homemade, we pass to the furnishings of the richer merchants in the Northern cities and of the wealthier planters in Maryland, Virginia, and the Carolinas. But we cannot take the establishments of Wentworth, Hancock, Vassall, Faneuil, Cuyler, Morris, Carter, Beverley, Manigault, or Laurens as typical of conditions which prevailed in the majority of colonial homes. Some people had silver plate, mahogany, fine china, and copper utensils; others owned china, delftware, and furniture of plain wood, with perhaps a few silver spoons, a porringer, and an occasional mahogany chair and table; still others, and these by far the largest number, used only pewter, earthenware, and wooden dishes, with the simpler essentials, spinning wheel, flatirons, pots and kettles, lamps and candlesticks, but no luxuries. There was in addition, of course, the class of the hopelessly poor, but it was not large and need not be reckoned with here.

The average New England country household was a sort of self-sustaining unit which depended little on the world beyond its own gates. Its equipment included not only the usual chairs, beds, tables, and kitchen utensils and tableware but also shoemakers' tools and shoe leather — frequently tanned in the neighborhood and badly done as a rule, — surgeon's tools and apothecary stuff, salves and ointments, branding irons, pestle and mortar, lamps, guns, and perhaps a sword, harness and fittings, occasionally a still or a cider press, and outfits for carpentering and blacksmithing. The necessary utensils for use in the household or on the farm were more important than upholstery, carved woodwork, fine linen, or silver plate. Everywhere there were hundreds of families which concerned themselves little about ornament or design. They had no money to spend on unessentials, still

JOHN HANCOCK'S SOFA

In Pilgrim Hall, Plymouth, Mass.

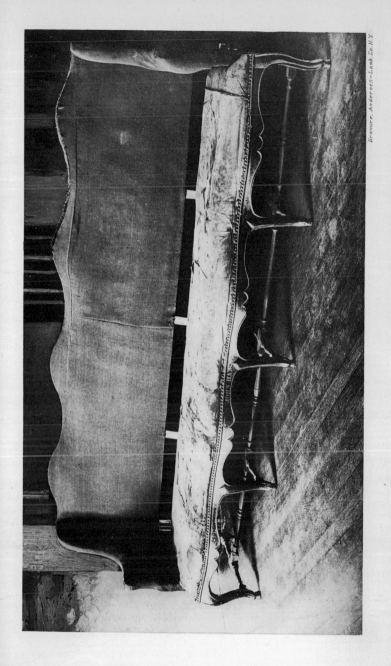

less on luxuries, and from necessity they used what they already possessed until it was broken or worn out; then, if it were not entirely useless, they repaired and patched it and went on as before. Economy and convenience made them use materials that were close at hand; and in many New England towns a familiar figure was the wood turner, who made plates and other utensils out of "dish-timber" as it was called, a white wood which was probably poplar or linden, but not basswood. Yet economical as these people were, even the unpretentious households possessed an abundance of mugs and tankards, which suggest their one indulgence and their enjoyment of strong drink.

As conditions of life improved and wealth increased, the number of those who were able to indulge in luxuries also increased. The period after 1730 was one of great prosperity in the colonies owing to the enlarged opportunities for making money which trade, commerce, and markets furnished. Though it was also a time of higher prices, rapid advance in the cost of living, and general complaint of the inadequacy of existing fees and salaries, those who were engaged in trade and had access to markets were able to indulge in luxuries which were unknown to the earlier settlers and which remained unknown to those living in the rural districts and on the frontier.

In the Northern cities and on Southern plantations costly and beautiful household furnishings appeared: furniture was carved and upholstered in leather and rich fabrics; tables were adorned with silver, china, and glassware; and walls were hung with expensive papers and decorated with paintings and engravings — all brought from abroad. A house thus equipped was not unlikely to contain a mahogany dining table capable of seating from fourteen to twenty persons, and an equal number of best Russia leather chairs, two of which would be arm or "elbow" chairs, double nailed, with broad seats and leather backs. Washington, for example, in 1757 bought "two neat mahogany tables $4\frac{1}{2}$ feet square when spread and to join occasionally," and "1 doz[n] neat and strong mahogany chairs," some with "Gothick arched backs," and one "an easy chair on casters." About the rooms were pieces of mahogany furniture of various styles, tea tables, card tables, candle stands, settees, and "sophas." On the walls, which were frequently papered, painted in color, or stenciled in patterns, hung family portraits painted by artists whose names are in many cases unknown to us, and framed pictures of hunting scenes, still life, ships, and humorous subjects, among which the engravings of Hogarth were always prime favorites. On the chimney breast, above the mantel, there was sometimes a scene or landscape, either painted directly on the wall itself or executed to order on canvas in England and brought to America. There were eight-day clocks and mantel clocks, and sconces, carved and gilt, upstairs and down. In the cupboard and on the sideboard would be silver plate in great variety and sets of best English china, ivory-handled knives and forks, glass in considerable profusion, though glassware, as a rule, was not much used, diaper tablecloths and napkins, brass chafing dishes, and steel plate warmers. There was always a centerpiece or épergne of silver, glass, or china.

In the bedrooms were pier glasses and bedsteads in many forms and colors, of mahogany and other woods. Frequently there were four-posters, with carved and fluted pillars and carved cornices or "cornishes," as they were generally spelled. The bedsteads were provided with hair mattresses and feather beds, woolen blankets, and linen sheets, and were adorned with silk, damask, or chintz curtains and valances. Russian gauze or lawn was used for mosquito nets, for mosquitoes were a great pest to the colonists.

On the large plantations there was to be found a great variety of utensils for kitchen, artisan, and farm use, most of which were brought from England, but some, particularly iron pots, axes, and scythes, from New England. For the kitchen there were hard metal plates, copper kettles and pans, pewter dishes in large numbers, chiefly for servants' use, yellow metal spoons, stone bottles, crocks, jugs, mugs, butter pots, and heavy utensils in iron for cooking purposes. For the farm there were grindstones, saws, files, knives, axes, adzes, planes, augurs, irons, hayrakes, carts, forks, reaping hooks, wheat sieves, spades, shovels, watering pots, plows, plowshares, and moldboards, harness and traces, harrows, ox chains, and scythes.

The farmer was thus provided with all the implements necessary for mowing, clearing underbrush, and cradling wheat, and all the other essential activities of an agricultural life. A wheel plow is mentioned as early as 1732, and in 1748 James Crokatt, an influential Charlestonian in England, sent over a plow designed to weed, trench, sow, and cover indigo, but of its construction we unfortunately know nothing. The colonists usually imported such articles as millstones, as large as forty-eight inches in diameter and fourteen inches thick, frog spindles and other parts for a tub mill or gristmill, hand presses, with lignum-vitæ rollers for cider, copper stills with sweat worms and a capacity as high as sixty gallons, vats for indigo, and pans for evaporating salt. For fishing there were plenty of rods, lines, hooks, seines with leads and corks, and eelpots. In addition to this varied equipment, nearly all the plantations had outfits for coopering, tanning, shoemaking, and other necessary occupations of a somewhat isolated community. Separate buildings were erected in which this artisan work was done, not only for the planter himself but also for his neighbors. Indeed the returns from this community labor constituted an important item in the annual statement of many a planter's income.

CHAPTER IV

HABILIMENTS AND HABITS

IN matters of dress, as well as in those of house building and furnishing, the eighteenth century was an era of greatly increased expenditure and costly display, of taste for luxuries and elaborate adornment, which not only involved the wealthier classes in extravagance beyond their resources but also ended far too often in heavy indebtedness and even in bankruptcy. Henry Vassall of Cambridge and William Byrd, 3d, of Virginia are examples of men who lived beyond their means and became in the end financially embarrassed. The years from 1740 to 1765 represent in the history of this country the highest point reached in richness of costume, variety of color, peculiarities of decoration, and excess of frills and furbelows on the part of both sexes. The richer classes affected no republican simplicity in the days before the Revolution, and while their standards did not prevail beyond town and tidewater, there were few who did not feel in some way, for good or for ill, this increasing complexity of the conditions of colonial life.

To deal systematically with the subject of dress in colonial times, we should trace its changes from the beginning, study the various forms it assumed according to the needs of climate and environment, and describe the clothing worn by all classes from the negro to the Governor and by all members of the family from the infant to the octogenarian. But a less formal account of colonial clothing will suffice to give one a fairly complete idea of what our ancestors wore as they went about their daily occupations and what they put on for such special occasions as weddings, funerals, assemblies, and social entertainments. It is also interesting to note the peculiar garb of such men as ministers, judges, sea captains, and soldiers; for the judge on the bench wore his robe of scarlet, the lawyer his suit of black velvet, and officials in office and representatives in the Assembly donned the habiliments suited to the occasion. The royal Governors were often gloriously bedecked, their councilors bewigged and befrilled, and Masons in procession to their lodges "wore their clothes," as one observer put it.

These, however, were not the everyday costumes of our forefathers. The majority of the colonists, except negroes and indentured servants, wore clothing which was relatively heavy and coarse. Throughout New England, and to a lesser extent elsewhere, men, women, and children wore homespun, with linen shirts, tow cloth skirts and breeches, and woolen stockings. When they bought materials, they selected heavy stuffs, such as fustian, kersey, sagathy, shalloon, duffel, drugget, and serge. By the middle of the century, however, farmers of the better class were wearing a finer quality of "shop goods," such as camblet, alamode, calamanco, and blue broadcloth. Perhaps the most widely used imported cloth was "ozenbrig," a tough, coarse linen woven in Osnabrück, Westphalia, which they made up into nearly everything from breeches and entire suits to sheets, table covers, and carpetbags. The village parson wore broadcloth when performing the duties of his office, and two suits of this material every six years was a fair average. For every day he wore the homespun of his parishioners. Buckskin and lambskin breeches were common; and deerskin, of which much of the clothing of our early ancestors was made, was later used for coats by those who were exposed to wind and weather. Stockings, which generally came over the knee, were blue, black, or gray, and might be of worsted, cotton, or cloth. Shoes, often of the coarsest kind, double-soled and made of cowhide, were made either at home or by village shoemakers who were also cobblers, or, after the middle of the century, at such towns as Lynn. A great many of the farming people, however, went barefoot in summer.

The New Englander usually possessed three suits of clothes: the durable and practical suit which he wore for working; a second-best which he put on for going to market or for doing errands in town; and his best which he reserved for the Sabbath-Day[1] and preserved with the utmost care. In both town and country, clothing was made at home by the women and help, or was cut out after the local fashion by the village tailor or seamstress, who brought shears and goose with them to the house, while the family provided material, thread, and board. Suits rarely fitted the wearer, alterations were common, and the same cloth was used for one member of the family after another until it

---

[1] People in New England always said Sabbath or Lord's Day; Sunday came in only late in the period among "the better sort."

was completely worn out. Patching and turning were evidences of thrift and economy.

Apprentices, indentured servants, and negroes in the North dressed in much the same way as did their "betters" but in clothes of poorer quality and cut, often made over from the discarded garments of their masters. In the South, what were called "plains" were imported in large quantities for the negroes, those in the house wearing blue jacket and breeches and those in the field generally white. Frequently the negroes worked with almost nothing on, and Josiah Quincy narrates how he was rowed over Hobcaw Ferry, in South Carolina, by six negroes, "four of whom had nothing on but their kind of breeches, scarce sufficient for covering."[1] When a servant or negro ran away, he put on everything that he had or could steal, and such a fugitive must have been a grotesque sight. One runaway servant is described as wearing a gray rabbit-skin hat with a clasp to it, a periwig of bright brown hair, a close serge coat, breeches of a brownish color, worsted stockings, and wooden-heeled shoes. One apprentice ran away wearing an old brown drugget coat and a pair of leather breeches and carrying in addition two ozenbrig

[1] Quincy, *Southern Journal*, 1773.

shirts and two pairs of trousers of the same material. An escaped negro was advertised as dressed
in shirt, jacket, and breeches, woolen stockings,
old shoes, and an old hat, and wearing a silver jewel
in one of his ears. Earrings or bobs in one or both
ears were frequent negro adornments.

The steady advance toward more ornate and
picturesque dress which began to be evident in
colonial life was due to closer contact with the West
Indies and the Old World. The Puritans had begun as early as 1675 to protest against the follies of
dress. Roger Wolcott of Connecticut, in his memoir written in 1759, speaks with regret of early
times in the colony and bewails the loss of the simplicity and honesty which the people had when he
was a boy. Toward the end of the seventeenth
century, he says, "their buildings were good to
what they had been, but mean to what they are
now; their dress and diet mean and coarse to what
it is now," and their regard for the Sabbath and
reverence for the magistrates far greater than in his
day. To the Quaker also the growing worldliness
of the times was a cause of depression and lament.
Peckover, writing of his travels in 1742, though
proud that the Quakers in the neighborhood of
Annapolis were accounted "pretty topping people

in the world," nevertheless regretted that they took so much liberty "in launching into finery," and believed that some of the children went "in apparel much finer and more untruthlike than most I ever saw in England." The richer planters and merchants not only wore foreign fabrics but deliberately copied foreign fashions. Eddis, writing from Annapolis in 1771, was of the opinion that a new fashion was adopted in America even earlier than in England, and he saw very little difference "in the manner of a wealthy colonist and a wealthy Briton."

A thousand and one articles from the great manufacturing towns of England — London, Bristol, Birmingham, Sheffield, Nottingham, Liverpool, Manchester, Torrington, and other centers — were brought in almost every ship that set sail for America. Scarcely a letter went from a Virginia planter or a Boston, New York, or Philadelphia merchant which did not contain a personal order for articles of clothing for himself or his family, and scarcely a captain sailed for England who did not carry commissions of one kind or another. The very names of the fabrics which the colonists bought show the extent of this early trade: Holland lawn, linen, duck, and blankets, German serge,

Osnaburg linen, Mecklenburg silk, Barcelona silk handkerchiefs, Flanders thread, Spanish poplin, Russian lawn and sheeting, Hungarian stuff, Romal or Bombay handkerchiefs, Scottish tartans and cloths, and Irish linen.

Colonel Thomas Jones in 1726 sent in one order for four pairs of " stagg" breeches, one fine Geneva serge suit, one fine cloth suit lined with scarlet, one fine drab cloth coat and breeches, one gray cloth suit, a drugget coat and breeches, a frieze coat, and several pairs of calamanco breeches and cloth breeches with silver holes. William Beverley, at different times, ordered a plain suit of very fine cloth, a summer suit of some other stuff than silk, with stocks to match, a winter riding suit, a suit of superfine unmixed broadcloth, a pair of riding breeches with silk stockings, a great riding coat, three Holland waistcoats with pockets, round-toed pumps, a pair of half jack boots, a beaver hat without stiffening, a light colored bobwig, knit hose to wear under others, and many pairs of kid and buckskin gloves. Later, he sent back the hose, "damnified in the voyage," to be dyed black and another pair that were too large in the calf, "I having but a slender body as you know by my measure." He also found fault with the boots, remarking, "I am but slender and my leg is not short."

For his wife Beverley ordered a suit of lutestring appropriate for a woman of forty years, a whale-bone coat, a hoop coat, a sarsenet quilted coat of any color but yellow, white tabby stays, a suit of "drest night cloaths or a mob, ruffles, and hand-kerchief," pairs of calamanco shoes, flowered stuff damask shoes, and silk shoes with silk heels, col-ored kid gloves and mittens, straw hats, thread, worsted, and pearl-colored silk hose, paduasoy rib-bons, and crewels for embroidering suit patterns. For his daughter he wished a whole Holland frock, a plain lutestring coat, a genteel suit of flowered silk cloth or "whatever is fashionable," a quilted petticoat, a cheap, plain riding habit, a head-dress, but if head-dresses were no longer fashionable then a mobcap with ribbons. For other children he wanted calamanco or silk shoes in considerable variety, sometimes ordering fine thin black calf-skins or skins of white leather to be made up into children's shoes on the plantation, hats with sil-ver laces, colored hose, and colored gloves. Even members of the fair sex tried their own hand at foreign purchase, for we are told that Sarah Bul-finch of Boston sent five pounds sterling in silver and one pound seventeen shillings in pennies to pay for purchases in London by a captain who was to buy the goods himself or to send the order to some London merchant.

Such an account of purchases could easily be extended, but enough has been said to show the general character of the orders and the dependence of the colonial planter and his family on the captain or the English merchant for fit, style, and color. The suits, which were made as a rule in London by a special tailor or dressmaker who had the measures, could never be tried on or fitted beforehand nor could their suitability in the matter of color and style be determined with any degree of satisfaction. The English correspondents in their letters interspersed their comments on trade with frequent suggestions regarding dress and fashions, and one remarked, for example, that "the French heads are little wore, mostly English, the hoops very small, upper petticoats of but four yards, the gowns unlined." These old country correspondents and the obliging captains must at times have indulged in some puzzling shopping expeditions in London. Orders for a hat, "genteel but not very gay," and for hats and shoes for children of certain ages but with the material and shape unspecified would call for the exercise of considerable discretion on a man's part,[1] and one is not surprised that complaints usually followed the receipt of the goods in America. Stockings were said to be too large, boots too small, hats too stiff or too soft or wrongly trimmed, leather rotten, and quality, colors, and patterns different from what was wanted. Only to those who frequented the colonial stores where pattern books sent from England were to be found was satisfaction guaranteed. Goods were often damaged on the voyage, and Beverley once wrote, "Goods received last spring damnified and (to cap the climax) have filled my house with cockroaches."

[1] That men shopped in America as well as in England appears from the following letter sent by a New England minister to his betrothed one week before the wedding:

"MADAM:

"I received a line from you by Mrs. Shepard with your request of purchasing a few small articles. I have bought 3¼ dozen of limes — and gauze for ruffles, but not plain. I asked Miss Polly Chase which was the most fashionable and best for Ladies ruffles and she told me that pink ruffled gauze was preferable, — and as she is acquainted with such little feminine matters, I bought what she recommended, and hope it will please you. I have got no edging for trimming them because there is no need of it with such flowered gauze. I have got some narrow silk ribbon to trim your apron with, but I did not know whether it should be white or black, nor what kind of an Apron you were about to trim. But I hope I have got that which will be agreeable to your gauze, or whatever your apron is to be made of." (From a MS in private hands.)

SILK BROCADE DRESS, WITH SILVER LACE STOMACHER

Worn by Mrs. Mary (Lynde) Oliver, of Salem, about 1765. In the Essex Institute, Salem, Mass.

PORTRAIT OF ELIZABETH WENSLEY

Born in Plymouth, Mass., in 1641, showing the head-dress, stomacher, and puffed sleeves of the period of about 1660–1670. Painting in Pilgrim Hall, Plymouth, Mass.

WOOL BROCADE DRESS

Worn by Dorothy, granddaughter of Governor Leverett of Massachusetts, at her wedding in 1719, to Major John Denison, of Ipswich. In the Essex Institute, Salem, Mass.

SILK BROCADE DRESS, WITH SILVER LACE STOMACHER

Worn by Mrs. Mary (Lynde) Oliver, of Salem, about 1765. In the
Essex Institute, Salem, Mass.

PORTRAIT OF ELIZABETH WENSLEY

Born in Plymouth, Mass., in 1644, showing the head-dress, stomacher, and puffed sleeves of the period of about 1660–1670. Painting
in Pilgrim Hall, Plymouth, Mass.

WOOL BROCADE DRESS

Worn by Dorothy, granddaughter of Governor Leverett of Massachusetts, at her wedding in 1719, to Major John Denison, of Ipswich.
In the Essex Institute, Salem, Mass.

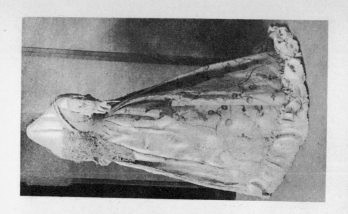

Bravure, Anderson — Lamb, Lu.N.Y.

The colors worn by the men were often varied
and bright. Cuyler of New York ordered a suit of
superfine scarlet plush, with shalloon and all trimmings, a coat and vest of light blue hair plush with
all trimmings, and fine shalloon suitable for each.
One merchant wanted a claret-colored duffel, another a gay broadcloth coat, vest, and breeches,
and still another two pieces of colored gingham
for a summer suit. All clothes, even those which
were fairly simple and worn by people of moderate
means, were adorned with buttons made of brass
and other metals, pearl, or cloth covered.

In addition to damask and silk stuffs, the women
wore calico and gingham printed in checks, patterns, and figures — dots, shells, or diamonds —
which on one occasion Stephen Collins complained
were too large and flaunting to suit the Philadelphia market.   Sometimes a pattern was stamped
on the cloth in London and was worked with crewel
or floss in the colonies. Women's hats were made
of silk or straw, their hoods of velvet or silk, and
their stockings of silk thread, cotton, worsted,
and even "plush." Shoes were often very elaborate, with uppers of silk or damask, and those for
girls were made of leather — calfskin, kid, or mo-
rocco — with silver laces and heels of wood covered

6

with silk. Gloves, which were worn from infancy to old age partly for reasons of fashion and partly to preserve the whiteness of the skin, were sometimes imported and sometimes made by the local tailor, who like the blacksmith was a craftsman of many accomplishments.

As for minor adornments, the ladies carried fans and wore girdles with buckles; but as a rule they possessed little jewelry except necklaces and a variety of finger rings either of plain gold or set with diamonds or rubies, and an occasional thumb ring. The men also wore rings, commonly bearing a seal of carnelian cut with the wearer's arms or some other device. Many of the mourning rings were realistically made with death's heads. As can be seen from the advertisements of the jewelers, the wearing of jewelry became much more common after 1750, earrings appeared, and even knee buckles and shoe buckles tended to become very ornate.

Underwear and lingerie in the modern sense were almost unknown and, though "nightgowns" are mentioned, it is uncertain whether they were designed for sleeping purposes or, as is more likely, for dressing gowns or my lady's toilet. For outside wear for the men there were great coats; and for the women coats and mantillas, often scarlet and blue; and for children, older folk, and soldiers, there were splatterdashes, a legging made of black glazed linen and reaching to the knee to protect the stockings. Men wore oilcloth capes when traveling in the rain, and the women put on a protective petticoat, sometimes called a weather skirt, and wore clogs or pattens against the mud. Umbrellas are mentioned early in the century, but they were probably only carriage tops, awnings, or sunshades. Parasols were used by a few, but sunbonnets — calashes — were customary on sunny days. Wigs were worn by men of all ranks, even by servants, and wig and peruke makers were to be found in all the large towns. Wig blocks frequently appear among the invoices, and before the queue came in many of the fashionable folk used bags for the hair. Lasts for making shoes, liquid blacking, and shoebrushes as well as hairbrushes were usually imported.

In traveling, men carried clean shirts, waistcoats, and caps, and — most interesting of all — clean sheets, but only occasionally clean stockings and handkerchiefs. Soap was frequently included in invoices, much of it made in New England. All Southern plantations had soap houses, with large copper vessels and other utensils in which soap was made for laundry purposes. Wash balls were imported possibly for domestic use, but they were also an important part of the barber's outfit. Men had their own razors and hones and shaved themselves, but those of the richer classes either went to the barber, at so much a quarter, or had the barber come to their houses.

Of indoor bathing it is difficult to find any trace. There were bathing pools on some of the Southern plantations, and swimming holes abounded then as now, but probably bathtubs were entirely unknown and "washing" was as far as the colonists' ablutions went.

The toothbrush had not yet been invented, but tooth washes and tooth powders were in use as early as 1718. We read, for instance, of the Essence of Pearl, guaranteed to do everything for the teeth; of the Dentium Conservator; and of another preparation, of which the name is not given but which was to be rubbed on with a cloth once a day, with the injunction, however, that "if you'd preserve their beauty use it only twice a week." Salt and water was the commonest dentifrice. That these prophylactics were not very successful is evident from the prevalent toothache and decay which necessitated frequent pulling and an early resort to false teeth. There were many individuals in the colonies who made such teeth and fastened them in, though dentistry was as yet hardly a vocation by itself. The apothecaries, the doctors, and even the barbers pulled teeth, and some of them posed as dentists. The goldsmiths advertised false teeth for sale. Spectacles or "spactickels," as one writer spells them, were ordinarily used when necessary, and ear trumpets were occasionally resorted to by the deaf.

Interesting and picturesque as are these manifold details of household equipment and personal use in the old colonial days, it is the color and energy of the daily life of the people of that time which make a deeper appeal to the reader of the twentieth century. Among the poorer colonists, who composed nine-tenths of the colonial population, life was a humdrum round of activities on the farm and in the shop. In the houses of the rich, women concerned themselves with their household duties, dress, and embroidery of all kinds. In some instances they managed the estate, engaged in business, and even took part in politics. In the towns many of the retail stores were conducted by women. Ruth Richardson of Talbot County, Maryland, carried on her husband's affairs after his death, and Martha Custis, before her marriage with George Washington, continued the correspondence and administered the plantation of her first husband, who died in 1757. Madam Smith, wife of the second landgrave, was another famous manager. In 1732, Mrs. Andrew Galbraith of Donegal, Pennsylvania, took part in her husband's political campaign, mounted her favorite mare, Nelly, and with a spur at her heel and her red cloak flying in the wind scoured the country from one end to the other. Needless to say, Andrew was elected.

Colonial marriages took place at even so early an age as fourteen; and the number of men and women who were married two, three, and four times was large. Instances of a thrice widower marrying a twice or thrice widow are not uncommon. Girls thus became the mothers of children before they were out of their 'teens. Sarah Hext married Dr. John Rutledge when she was fourteen and was the mother of seven children before she was twenty-five. Ursula Byrd, who married Robert Beverley, had a son and died before she was seventeen; Sarah Breck was only sixteen or seventeen when she married Dr. Benjamin Gott; Sarah Pierrepont was seventeen when she married

Jonathan Edwards; and Hannah Gardiner was of the same age when she married Dr. McSparran. Large families, even of twenty-six children of a single mother, are recorded, but infant mortality was very great. John Coleman and Judith Hobby had fourteen children, of whom five died at birth, and only four grew up and married, one to the well-known Dr. Thomas Bulfinch of Boston. Though Sarah Hext lived to be sixty-eight, many mothers died early, and often in childbirth. An instance is given of a burying ground near Bath, Maine, in which there were the graves of ten married women, eight of whom had died between the ages of twenty-two and thirty, probably as the result of large families and overwork. Second marriages were the rule, though probably few were as sudden as that of the Sandemanian, Isaac Winslow, who proposed to Ben Davis's daughter on the eve of the day he buried his wife and married her within a week.

The marriage ceremony generally took place at home instead of in the church, and in many of the colonies was followed by a bountiful supper, cards, and dancing. There were often bridesmaids, diamond wedding-rings, and elaborate hospitality. In New England the festivities lasted two or three days and visitors stayed a week. In the South one proposing to marry had to give bond that the marriage would not result in a charge on the community, and usually the banns were read three times in meeting and a license was obtained and recorded. In Virginia, where the county clerks granted licenses, children under age could not marry without the consent of their parents, and indentured servants could not marry during their servitude. In Connecticut the banns were published but once and protests against a marriage were affixed to the signpost or the church door. Blanks for licenses were distributed by the Governor and could be obtained of the local authorities. A curious custom was that of "bundling" (sometimes also called "tarrying," though the practices seem to have been different), which Burnaby describes as putting the courting couple into bed with garments on to prevent scandal, when "if the parties agree, it is all very well; the banns are published and [the two] are married without delay." Another curious custom, which prevailed from New England to South Carolina, made the second husband responsible for the debts of the first, unless the bride were married in her chemise in the King's Highway. In one instance the lady stood in a closet and extended her hand through the door, and in another, well authenticated, both chemise and closet were dispensed with.

Divorces were rare: the Anglican Church refused to sanction them, and the Crown forbade colonial legislatures to pass bills granting them. The matter was therefore left to the courts. As New England courts refused to break a will, so, as a rule, they refused to grant a divorce, though there are a number of exceptions, for divorces were allowed in both Massachusetts and Connecticut.[1] In the case of unhappy marriages, separation by mutual agreement was occasionally resorted to. Sometimes the lady ran away; and, indeed, advertisements for runaway wives seem almost as common in Southern newspapers as those for runaway servants. Marriages between colonial women and English officials, missionaries of the Society for the Propagation of the Gospel, and even occasional visitors from abroad were not infrequent. Sir William Draper, Knight of the Bath, who made an American tour in 1770, wooed and won during his journey Susanna, daughter of Oliver De Lancey of New York.

[1] "I was at court al day about geting Sister Mary divorced & obtained it." Hempstead, *Diary*, p. 147.

Family life in the colonies was full of affection, though the expression of feeling was usually restrained and formal. Colonel Thomas Jones, for example, addressed his fiancée, Elizabeth Cocke — a widow, and a niece of Mark Catesby the naturalist — as "Madam" or "Dearest Madam" during their engagement, though after their marriage his greeting was "My dearest Life." One of his wife's letters the gallant and devoted Jones read over "about twenty times," and his correspondence with her contains such gems of solicitude as this: "If my heart could take a flight from the imprisonment of a worthless carcasse little better than durt, it should whisper to you in your slumbers the truth of my soul, that you may be agreeably surprised with the luster of cœlestial visions surrounding you on every side with presents of joy and comfort in one continued sleep, till the sparkling rays of the sun puts you in mind with him to bless the earth with your presence." Richard Stockton, writing to his wife Emilia from London in 1760, said that he had "been running to every American coffee-house to see if any vessels are bound to your side of the water," and added: "I see not an obliging tender wife but the image of my dear Emilia is full in view; I see not a haughty,

imperious, and ignorant dame but I rejoice that
the partner of my life is so much the opposite."

Affection for children was not often openly expressed in New England, though ample testimony
shows that it existed. Children were repressed in
mind as well as in body, and their natural and
youthful spirits were generally ascribed to original
sin. Toward their parents their attitude was de-
corous in the extreme. Deborah Jeffries addressed
her father as "Hon^d Sir" and wrote: "I was much
pleased to hear my letters were agreeable to you
and mama, I shall always do my endeavour to
please such kind and tender parents." Education
and punishment in colonial days went frequently
hand in hand, and servants and children were often
treated with extreme harshness. Whipping was the
universal remedy for misbehavior and was resorted
to on all occasions in the case of children in their
early years, of servants throughout the period of
their indenture, and of negroes during their whole
lives. Yet one cannot read Colonel Jones's reference to "these two dear pledges of your love," in a
letter to his wife, or William Beverley's lament for
his son who died, as he thought, for lack of care
when away from home, without realizing the depth
of parental love in colonial times.

Sickness, death, and the frailties of human life were perennial subjects of conversation and correspondence and few family letters of those days were free from allusions to them. From infancy to old age death took ample toll — so great was the colonial disregard for the laws of sanitation, so little the attention paid to drainage and disinfection. The human system was dosed and physicked until it could hold no more. Governor Ogle of Maryland said of his predecessor that he took more physic than any one he had ever known in his life, and Maria Byrd was accustomed to swallow "an abundance of phynite," whatever that was. Every home had its medicine chest, either made up in England at Apothecaries' Hall or supplied by some near-by druggist, who furnished the necessary "chymical and galenical medicines." Joseph Cuthbert of Savannah, for example, fitted up boxes of medicines, with directions for use on the plantation. Medicinal herbs were dispensed by Indian doctors, and popular concoctions were taken in large doses by credulous people. Madam Smith wrote that the juice of the Jerusalem oak had cured all the negro children on the plantation of a distemper and that several negroes had drunk as much as half a pint of it at a time. Nostrums, quack remedies, and proprietary medicines made by a secret formula were very common. We read of Ward's Anodyne Pearls to be worn as necklaces by children at teething time, of the Bezoar stone for curing serpent bites, of Seneca Snake Root, Bateman's Pectoral Drops, Turlington's Original Balsam, Duffy's Elixir, Countess Kent's Powder, Anderson's Pills, Boerhaave's Chymical Tincture, and other specifics to be given in allopathic doses. Jesuits' bark, salt wormwood, sweet basil, iron, treacle, calomel, flos unguent, sal volatile salts, and rhubarb were on the family lists; and here and there were resorts where people drank medicinal waters or used them for bathing.

The prominent place which death occupied in colonial thought and experience gave to funerals the character of social functions and public events. They were objects of general interest and were usually attended by crowds of people. Children were allowed to attend, often as pallbearers, that they might be impressed with the significance of death as the inevitable end of a life of trial and probation. Everywhere, before the reaction of the sixties, funerals were occasions of expense and extravagant display. It was unusual to find Robert Hume of Charleston declaring in his will that his funeral should not cost over ten pounds, that the coffin should be plain and not covered by a pall, and that none of his relatives should wear mourning. Occasionally a colonist expressed the wish to be buried without pomp or funeral sermon, but such a preference was rare. The giving of gloves, rings, and scarves was provided for in nearly every will, and it is easy to believe the report that some of the clergy accumulated these articles by the hundred. Drinking, even to the point of intoxication, at funerals became such a scandal that ministers in New England thundered at the practice from the pulpit, and Edmund Watts in Virginia was moved to declare in his will that "no strong drinke be provided or spent" when he was buried. But the custom was too deep seated to be easily eradicated.

The dead were buried in the burying ground or churchyard, though private burial places were customary on the plantations and in many parts of northern New York and New England. At Annapolis a lot in the churchyard was leased at a nominal rent, but interment within the church was allowed for a consideration which was possible only to people of wealth and which went to the rector. A potter's field seems hardly to have been known in colonial times, for we are told that the poorer classes and negroes in Baltimore buried their "deceased relations and acquaintances in several streets and allies" of the town, and that not until 1792 was a special section set apart for their use. A suicide was interred at a crossroads and a stake was driven through the body. Usually, except among the Quakers, stones, table monuments, and headpieces were erected over the dead and often bore elaborate and curious inscriptions and carvings more or less crude. The commonest materials, freestone, syenite, and slate, were usually quarried in the colonies, though marble was always brought from England. Martha Custis procured in London a marble tomb for her first husband, and William Beverley directed that a stone of this material be imported for his father's grave. Vaults were constructed by those who could afford them and were widely used in the North in the eighteenth century.

CHAPTER V

EVERYDAY NEEDS AND DIVERSIONS

THERE was no want of food in colonial households and little scarcity or threatened famine in
the land of our forefathers. Though the Southern
and West Indian colonists paid but little attention
to the raising of the more important food staples,
they were able to obtain an adequate supply
through channels of distribution which remained
almost unchanged throughout the colonial period.
The provisions of New England and the flour, beef,
pork, and peas of New York and Pennsylvania
were carried wherever they were wanted and satisfied the demands of those who were otherwise absorbed in the cultivation of tobacco, rice, indigo,
and sugar. The greatest difficulty lay in the pres-
ervation of perishable foods, for the colonists had
as yet no adequate means of keeping fresh their
meats and provisions. In the outlying districts,
where supplies were irregular, many a family lived

on smoked, salted, and pickled foods and during the winter were entirely without the fresh meats and green vegetables which were available in the summer and autumn seasons. [1]

This need was partly satisfied by the plentiful supply of venison obtained from the forests, for the colonists were great hunters. Fowling pieces, powderflasks. shot bags, worms, and ramrods were a part of every country householder's equipment. Though deer and wild birds were less plentiful in the eighteenth than in the seventeenth century, their number was still large; and wild turkeys, geese, pigeons, hares, and squirrels were always to be found. Fish abounded in the rivers; lobsters were obtainable off the shores in considerable numbers; clams were always plentiful; and oysters were eaten not only along the seacoast from Maine to Georgia but even in the back country as far as the Shenandoah, whither they were sent packed in old

---

[1] Just when and where ice first began to be housed for summer use it is difficult to discover but the following extract from a manuscript journal of Epaphrus Hoyt, who journeyed from Deerfield to Philadelphia and back in 1790, is suggestive. Writing on the 6th of August, he said: "After we got through Hell Gate we drunk a bowl of Punch made with Ice which Mr. Yates a passenger had took on board at N. York. This was very curious to see Ice at this season of the year — which is kept (as Mr. Yates informed us) through the summer in houses built on purpose."

barrels and flour casks "lest the waggoners get foul of 'em." Turtles caught in the neighborhood or sent from the West Indies were frequently served up on the tables of the richer families in all the colonies. Even buffalo steaks were eaten, for John Rowe records a dinner in 1768 at which venison, buffalo steaks, perch, trout, and salmon were placed before the guests.

Nearly all the meats, vegetables, and fruits familiar to housekeepers of today were known to the colonial dames. In the better houses, beef, mutton, lamb, pork, ham, bacon, and smoked and dried fish were eaten, as well as sausages, cheese, and butter, which were usually homemade in New England, though in the Middle Colonies and the South cheese was frequently imported from Rhode Island. It is related that once when Beekman of New York could not sell some Rhode Island cheese that "was loosing in weight and spoiling with maggots," he proposed to have it hawked about the town by a cartman. As for vegetables, the New Englander was familiar with cabbages, radishes, lettuce, turnips, green corn carrots, parsnips, spinach, onions, beets, parsley savory, mustard, peppergrass, celery, cauliflower, squashes, pumpkins, beans, peas, and asparagus; but only the

more prosperous householders pretended to culti-
vate even a majority of these in their gardens.
In the rural districts, only cabbages, beans, pumpkins, and other vegetables of the coarser varieties were grown. Potatoes were not introduced
until after the advent of the Scotch-Irish in 1720,
and they did not for some time become a common
vegetable. Dr. McSparran of Rhode Island made
a record in his diary in 1743 that potatoes were
being dug, and Birket speaks of them as being
"plentifully produced" by the year 1750. Toma-
toes were hardly yet deemed edible, and only
an occasional mention of cucumbers can be
found. In the South sweet potatoes early became
popular, and watermelons and muskmelons were
raised in large quantities, though they were grown
in the North also to some extent. Every Southern plantation, notably in Virginia, had its vegetable and flower garden, and familiar items in the
lists of articles ordered from England are the seeds
and roots which the planter wanted.

Fruit was abundant everywhere. Apples, pears,
peaches, apricots, damsons, plums, quinces, cher-
ries, and crab apples were all raised in the orchards, North and South, while oranges, probably small and very sour, were grown in South

Carolina and on Governor Grant's plantation in East Florida. English and Italian gardeners were employed by certain of the wealthier planters and often exhibited superior skill in matters of grafting and propagating plants and shrubs.[1] At first grafts were obtained from England and the Continent, but as early as 1735 Paul Amatis started his "Georgian Nursery" in South Carolina, and later William Prince established in the North a large fruit nursery at Flushing, Long Island, where he said that he had fifteen thousand trees fit to remove, "all innoculated and grafted from bearing trees." Christian Leman began a similar nursery at Germantown, Pennsylvania. Of the smaller fruits, strawberries, blackberries, and gooseberries were cultivated and highly prized; wild strawberries and huckleberries were as well known as they are now; and grapes were found in enormous quantities in a wild state, though efforts to grow vineyards for the purpose of making wine were never very successful.

In preparing vegetables and fruits for preserving, both for the winter's supply at home and the

[1] Grafting was practiced in New England at an early date. The Reverend Joseph Green of Salem says in his diary, that on April 17, 1701, he grafted 59 "cyons" on 24 trees. Essex Institute *Historical Collections*, vol. VIII, p. 220.

Southern and West India markets, the New England housewives proved themselves eminently resourceful and skillful. They pickled Indian corn and other vegetables, nuts, and oysters; they dried apples or else made them into sauce and butter; and they preserved fruits not in cans or sealed jars but in huge crocks covered with paper and so sealed that the fruit would keep for a long time without fermenting.

For spices and condiments, however, all the colonists had to depend on outside sources. Capers, English walnuts, anchovies, nutmegs, pepper, mace, cloves, cinnamon, ginger, olives, salad oil, almonds, raisins, and dried currants were commonly ordered from England; lemons, which in 1763 were declared to have become "almost a necessity for the health and comfort of the inhabitants of North America," were obtained from the Mediterranean and the West Indies; coffee, tea (hyson, bohea, congo, and green), and "cocoa nuts"[1] came from England usually, though much of the spice, tea, and cocoa was smuggled in from Amsterdam or the foreign West Indies. From the latter came also sweetmeats, tamarinds, preserved

[1] The eighteenth-century name for the cocoa bean from which chocolate is made.

ginger, citrons, and limes, which were often brought by the sea captains as presents from West India merchants, to whom hams, turkeys, geese, and the like were sent in return. Spices and coffee were ground at home, and "cocoa nuts" were made into chocolate, either at home or at a neighboring mill. Beverley ordered a stone and roller for preparing chocolate on his plantation, and in New England there were several chocolate mills, where the beans were crushed either for the housewife at her request or for sale.

In the country households of the North nearly everything for the table was obtained from the farm, and only salt, sugar, and spices were bought. Even sugar was a luxury; maple sugar, honey, and brown muscovado sugar were sometimes used, but the common sweetening was molasses, though this was rejected in the South for table use. The food, though ample in quantity, was lacking in variety and was heavier and less appetizing than in the cities. The commonest dishes were pork, smoked salmon, red herring, cod, mackerel, Indian meal in many forms, vegetables (including the familiar "succotash"), pies, and puddings. But in the Northern cities the variety was greater and equaled that of the South. Philadelphia had scores of families whose elaborate tables seemed a sinful waste to John Adams, who has recorded in his diary the luxury of the Quaker households. In Massachusetts the extravagance of hospitality was none the less marked. Henry Vassall's expense book mentions oysters, herrings, mackerel, salmon, sausages, cheese, almonds, biscuit, ducks, chickens, turkeys, fowls, quails, teals, pigeons, beef, calf's head, rabbit, lamb, veal, venison, and quantities of vegetables and fruit, as well as honey, chocolate, and lemons.

In Virginia breakfast, at least, was a less elaborate meal than in New England. Harrower tells us that at Belvidera it consisted of tea, coffee, or chocolate, warm bread, butter, and cold meat. Eddis mentions a Maryland breakfast "of tea, coffee, and the usual accompaniments, ham, dried venison, beef, and other relishing articles." Dinner, which was always served at noon, consisted at Belvidera of "smoack'd bacon or what we call pork ham . . . either warm or cold; when warm we have also either warm roast pigg, lamb, ducks, or chicken, green pease or anything else they fancy." As these colonists also had "plenty of roast and boyled and good strong beer," it is perhaps not to be wondered at that they "but seldom eat any

supper." Fithian speaks of a "winter plan" at
Nomini Hall, with coffee " just at evening" and
supper between eight and nine o'clock. Quincy
gives an account of his entertainment at Charleston which is full of interest. "Table decent but not
inelegant; provisions indifferent, but well dressed;
good wines and festivity." And again on other occasions, "a prodigious fine pudding made of what
they call rice flour. Nicknacks brought on table
after removal of meats," "a most genteel supper,"
"a solid plentiful good table." What most impressed him were the superior quality of the wines,
the frequent exchange of toasts, and the presence of
musicians. Adam Gordon said of Charleston that
the poultry and pork were excellent, the beef and
mutton middling, and the fish very rare and expensive. "All the poor," he added, "and many of
the rich eat rice for bread and give it even a preference; they use it in their cakes, called Journey
Cakes, and boiled, or else boiled Indian corn, which
they call Hominy."

It is a well-known fact that the colonists were
heavy drinkers and that they consumed liquors
of every variety in enormous quantities on all
important occasions — baptisms, weddings, funerals, barn raisings, church raisings, house raisings,

ship launchings, ordinations, perambulations, or "beating the bounds," at meetings of commissions and committees, and in taverns, clubs, and private houses. In New England a new officer was expected on training day "to wet his commission bountifully." Among the New England farmers beer, cider, cider brandy, and rum were the ordinary beverages. Cider, however, gradually supplanted beer, and the thrifty farmer sometimes laid in for the winter a supply of from ten to thirty barrels. A keg or puncheon of rum would usually lie alongside the barrels of cider in the cellar. There it would be left to ripen with age, with the assistance of about five dozen apples, peeled and cut in pieces, which were added to improve the flavor. Beer was brewed at home by the wives or in breweries in some of the towns; even Charleston experimented in brewing with malt from Philadelphia. Ale and small beer in bottles were imported from England; and spruce beer was used as a drink and sometimes at sea as a remedy against scurvy.

Rum was distilled in all the leading New England towns, notably at Boston and Newport. Not only was it drunk at home and served out as a regular allowance to artisans and workmen, but it was also used in trade with the Indians, in dealings with the fishermen off Nova Scotia and Newfoundland, in exchange with the Southern Colonies for grain and naval stores, and in the purchase of slaves in Africa.[1] Rum from the West Indies was always more highly prized than that of New England and brought a higher price in the market.

Though in all the colonies rum was a common drink and arrack was consumed also to some extent on Southern tables, the colonists in the North were more addicted to both these drinks than were the Southerners, and the colonists in New England more than those in New York and Pennsylvania, where beer drinking predominated among the Dutch and the Germans. On Southern plantations the large number of distilleries which existed and the presence of stillhouses, copper stills, and sweat worms indicate a wider activity than merely the distilling of rum from molasses. Quantities of apple and peach brandy, cherry fling, and cherry rum were made in Virginia and South Carolina, and we know that on one occasion Van Cortlandt

[1] In 1763 the merchants of Boston estimated that Massachusetts produced yearly 15,000 hogsheads or 1,500,000 gallons of rum, distributed as follows: 9000 hogsheads for home consumption and the whale, cod, and mackerel fisheries; 3000 for the Southern Colonies; 1700 for Africa; and 1300 for Nova Scotia and Newfoundland. These figures upset some time-honored calculations as to the amount of rum used in the slave trade.

of New York squared a single Virginia account by accepting six hundred gallons of peach brandy instead of cash. To a certain extent fruit brandies were made in the North also, but the famous apple-jack of New Jersey does not appear to have been introduced until just before the Revolution. It has been truly said that fruit growing in America "had its beginning and for almost two hundred years its whole sustenance in the demand for strong drink."

Of imported wines those most frequently in demand were madeira, claret, Canary vidonia, burgundy and other French wines, port, and brandy. A sort of homemade claret was prepared from wild grapes by the Huguenots at Manakintown, but it always remained an experiment. Claret was a table drink in New England, but Gerard Beekman wrote in 1753 that it was in no demand in New York and that French wines were not in favor. Though it was imported in considerable quantities, brandy never became a popular colonial drink, and in Charleston, when the price was high, it was used chiefly for medicinal purposes. In the same city, Canary vidonia was considered much inferior to madeira and was not usually liked because it was too sweet. Birket, however, said that it was a common drink among people of fortune in New England, though it was harsh in taste and inclined to look thick. As a rule the colonists did not like sweet wines, and for this reason the aromatic malmsey never pleased the colonial palate. Quincy, who found the Charleston wines "by odds the richest" he had ever tasted, thought them superior to those served by John Hancock of Boston and Henry Vassall of Cambridge. His account of the customary protracted toasting and drinking at Charleston tables reminds one of the story Hamilton is said to have related of Washington. "Gen'l H. told us," says London in his diary, "that Gen'l Washington notwithstanding his perfect regularity and love of decorum could bear to drink more wine than most people. He loved to make a procrastinated dinner — made it a rule to drink a glass of wine with every one at table and yet always drank 3–4 or more glasses of wine after dinner, according to his company — and every night took a pint of cream and toasted crust for supper."

An excellent idea of the customary drinks of these colonial times can be gained from a list issued in 1744 by the county court of Chowan, North Carolina, mentioning madeira, Canary vidonia, Carolina cider, Northern cider, strong malt beer of

American make, flip with half a pint of rum in it, porter from Great Britain, punch with loaf sugar, lime juice, and half a pint of rum, British ale or beer bottled and wired in Great Britain. Flip was made in different ways, but a common variety was a mixture of rum, pumpkin beer, and brown sugar, into which a red-hot poker had been plunged. For lighter drinks there were lemonade, citron water, distillations of anise seed, oranges, cloves, treacle, ratafia, peppermint, and angelica, and other home-made cordials and liqueurs.

Taverns, usually poor in appearance and service, were to be found everywhere from Maine to Georgia, in the towns, on the traveled roads, and at the ferry landings. They not only offered accommodations for man and beast but frequently served also for council and assembly meetings, social gatherings, merchants' associations, preaching, the acting of plays; and their balconies proved convenient for the making of public speeches and announcements. The taverns, which also provided resorts where it was possible for "gentlemen to enjoy their bowl and bottle with satisfaction," were the scenes of a vast amount of hard drinking and quarreling. It was, for instance, in a corner parlor of Hatheway's tavern in Charleston in 1770, that De Lancey was mortally wounded by Hadley in a duel fought with pistols in the dark. Men met at the taverns in clubs to play billiards and cards, to drink, and to gamble, and the following record shows the sort of score that they ran up: "Punch and game of billiards; one pack of cards; to flip at whick [whist]; to punch at ombre; ditto at all fours; to liquor at billiards all night; to sangaree and wine; to sack, punch, and beer; club to brandy punch; to two sangarees at billiards; to punch at cards, club afterwards." Many of the taverns had skittle alleys and shuffleboards, but neither these games nor billiards and bowling were confined to public resorts. Billiard tables were to be found in private houses, and bowling was often played in alleys specially built for the purpose; and we are told that Councilman Carter had a bowling green near Nomini Hall.

Card playing was a common diversion. Packs of cards must have come in with the first Virginia and Maryland settlers, for card tables are known to have been in use on Kent Island as early as 1658. The number of packs of cards imported was prodigious: one ship from London brought to the Cape Fear Colony toward the end of this period 144 packs, another 576, and another 888; a Boston invoice shows 1584 packs; a single Pennsylvania importation was valued at forty-four pounds sterling. We know that cards were distributed and sold in stores from Portsmouth and Albany to Charleston and as far back as the Shenandoah Valley, where Daniel Morgan, later a major general under Washington, spent his hilarious youth, drinking rum, playing cards, and running up gambling debts. From these facts we can appreciate what Peter du Bois meant when he wrote of his days at Wilmington: "I live very much retired for want of a social set, who will drink claret and smoke tobacco till four in the morning; the gentlemen of this town might be so if they pleased, but an intollerable itch for gaming prevails in all companies. This I conceive is the bane of society and therefore I shun the devotees to cards and pass my hours chiefly at home with my pipe and some agreeable author." Henry Laurens, a merchant, mentions the case of a young man in his counting-house, who had given his note to a card sharper and was with difficulty rescued from "the gaping pickpockets" who had "followed him like a shadow." Gaming for high stakes was a well-known failing of the Vassall family, and because of his love for reckless play Henry undoubtedly hastened his bankruptcy. But this vice was not confined to the quality, for negroes and street boys, from Salem to Charleston, gambled in the streets at "pawpaw" and dice; and "huzzlecap" or pitching pennies was so common as to call forth protests and grand jury presentments in an effort to abate what was justly deemed a public nuisance.

The use of tobacco was general in every class of society and in every locality. Even women of the lower classes smoked, for there is a reference to one who had a fit, dropped a "coal" from her pipe, and was burned to death. For smoking and chewing, tobacco was either cut and dried or else was made up into "pigtails," as the small twisted ropes or braids were called, though "paper tobacco," put up in paper packages, was coming into favor. Tobacco was smoked only in pipes, either the fine long glazed pipes of clay imported from England and commonly called "churchwardens," or in Indian pipes of red pipestone, often beautifully carved. Probably the Dutch and Germans continued to use in America their old-country porcelain pipes with pendulous stems, and it is more than likely that wooden and cob pipes were in fashion in the rural districts. Cigars were not known in America until after 1800. Though in early advertisements snuff was recommended as medicinal, the taking of snuff came to be as much a matter of social custom as of pleasure: to the rich merchant and planter the snuff-box was an article of decoration and its proper use a matter of etiquette. Snuff was usually imported in canisters and bladders and occasionally in bottles; but there were snuff factories in Philadelphia and New York, and the father of Gilbert Stuart was a snuff maker in Rhode Island.

In addition to the diversion to be obtained from drinking, smoking, and gambling, which may be called the representative colonial vices, there were plenty of amusements and sports which absorbed the attention of the colonists, North and South. The woods and waters offered endless opportunity in summer for fishing and in winter for such time-honored pursuits as hunting, fowling, trapping, and fishing through the ice. John Rowe of Boston was a famous and untiring fisherman; thousands of other enthusiasts played the part of colonial Isaak Waltons; and there was a fishing club on the Schuylkill as early as 1732. Fishing rods, lines, sinkers, and hooks were commonly imported from England.

The woods were full of such big game as elk, moose, black bears, deer, lynxes, pumas or panthers (sometimes called "tigers"), gray wolves, and wildcats; and there was an abundance of such smaller animals as foxes, beavers, martens or fishers, otters, weasels, minks, raccoons, and muskrats or "musquashes," as they are still called in rural New England. These animals were killed without regard for the future of the species. Sometimes the settlers even resorted to the wasteful and unsportsmanlike method of burning the forests, so that the larger animals began to disappear from the Eastern regions. Buffaloes, for instance, were formerly found in North Carolina as far east as Craven County, but in the upcountry of South Carolina it was said that three or four men with dogs could kill twenty of these animals in a day. In this same State the last elk had been killed as early as 1781. Nor was the case otherwise with the smaller game and fowl. Wooden decoys and camouflaged boats aided in the destruction of the ducks; caged pigeons were used to attract the wilder members of the species, which were shot in large numbers, particularly in New England; and so unlicensed had the destruction of the heath hen become in New York that in 1708 the province determined to protect its game by providing for a closed season. Thus early did the movement for conservation begin in America.

The sport of hunting led to the improvement of firearms and to the introduction of the English custom of fox-hunting. Guns, which had formerly been clumsy and unreliable, were now perfected to such a degree that we find references to a gun which would repeat six times, a chambered gun, a double-barreled gun, and a "neat birding piece, mounted with brass." Rifles, which were common, were used for target practice as well as for hunting. Rifle matches were arranged in Virginia on muster days, and in Connecticut shooting at a mark for a money prize was a favorite diversion on training days. Both the Virginians and the New Yorkers were skillful fox-hunters and very fond of riding to hounds, for which they imported their foxes from England.

In the South the two leading sports were horse racing and cockfighting, though the former was an absorbing passion in all the colonies. Cock-fighting — so well illustrated in Hogarth's famous engraving, which may well have been on many a colonial wall after 1760 — was a sport which had been brought to America from England and which had lost none of its brutality in the transfer. From Annapolis to Charleston the local rivalry was intense. We read, for example, that a main of cocks was fought between the gentlemen of Gloucester and those of James River, in which twenty pairs were matched and fought for five guineas the battle and fifty guineas the odd. When Gloucester won, James River challenged again and this time came out ahead, and so the contest went on. Matches were frequently advertised in the Annapolis, Williamsburg, and Charleston papers, stating in each case so many cocks, so many battles, so much each and so much the odd, in guineas, pounds, and pistoles. Champion cocks, like horses, were known by name and were pitted against all comers. Quincy saw five battles on his way from Williamsburg to Port Royal, and mentions having met in Maryland two persons " of the middling rank in life," who had spent three successive days in cockfighting and "as many nights in riot and debauchery."

Horse racing was even more engrossing than cockfighting. What is perhaps the earliest recorded race took place in York County, Virginia, in 1674, when a tailor and a physician had a brush with their horses, in consequence of which the tailor was fined by the county court, because "it was contrary to law for a labourer to make a race, being a sport only for gentlemen." Racing in

Virginia was thus enjoyed as an occasional pastime at a very early date, though it did not become a regular practice until after 1730, when the first blooded stallion was imported. Apparently the earliest race outside of Virginia occurred in East New Jersey in 1694, when Sam Jennings was charged with being drunk when riding a horse race with J. Slocum. It may be noted in passing that horse racing, gambling, and possessing a billiard table were forbidden by law in Connecticut and that all such pursuits were discouraged, though not forbidden, in Massachusetts and Rhode Island.[1]

Races were run on greens at Newmarket in New Hampshire, at Hempstead, Flatland Plains, and around Beaver Pond on Long Island, on John Vanderbilt's field on Staten Island, at Paulus Hook (now Jersey City), at Morristown and Perth Amboy in New Jersey, at Center Course near Philadelphia, and at Lancaster in the same colony, at the race course near Annapolis, at Alexandria, Fredericksburg, and many other places in Virginia. Races were also run on dozens of "race paths" in

---

[1] Horses were raced in Connecticut, but privately rather than publicly. Hempstead in his *Diary* (pp. 148, 156, 579, 601) mentions three races and one race horse.

North and South Carolina, where large plantations had their own courses, as well as on such public tracks as the Round Course at Monck's Corner, York Course at the Old Quarter House, and Thomas Butler's Race Ground on Charleston Neck.

The number of blooded stallions and mares in the colonies before the Revolution must have been very large. Massachusetts was the home of many blooded horses, Rhode Island was famous for its Narragansett pacers, and even Connecticut had stallions obtained from England for breeding purposes. Virginia alone, beginning her importation with Bully Rock in 1730, has record of fifty stallions and thirty mares bred from stock introduced from England, and the services of breeding horses were frequently advertised. The horses used for racing were, of course, runners and pacers, as the trotting horse had not yet been introduced, and the time which they made is recorded as low as two minutes. The fast colts of Governor Sharpe of Maryland were well known, and Governor Ogle had a famous imported horse named Spark. The Narragansett pacers, as they were called, were the most distinctive colonial breed, and horsemen from the Southern Colonies visited Rhode Island, purchased stock, and advertised the merits of their animals in the newspapers. Some of the colonial horse breeders preferred to buy their stock in England, and it is interesting to note, as an indication of the value of horses in those days, that Charles Carroll contemplated buying a stallion for one hundred pounds sterling and brood mares for fifty pounds each. It is perhaps equally interesting to know that he was dissuaded from his purchase by an inveterate colonial distrust of the ways of the mother country.

Horse races were of all kinds — for scrubs and thoroughbreds, three- or four-year-olds, colts, and fillies; the heats were generally the best two out of three; and the distance was from one to five miles, with entrance fees and double at the post, and prizes in the form of purses, silver punch bowls, pint pots and tankards, saddles, bridles, boots, jockey caps, and the like. There were such prizes, too, as the Jockey Club Plate, the Town Purse, and the Free Mason's Plate. There was a Jockey Club in Virginia before the Revolution, but that in Maryland was not organized until 1783. The crowds were large, the side betting was heavy, and pickpockets were always on hand. The jockeys, black or white, who rode the horses were sometimes thrown and seriously injured or killed. On at least one course a "ladies' gallery," or grand stand, was erected, and there were doubtless others else-where. So great was the popularity of these races that the Quaker Peckover had to wait until a Virginia race was over before he could hold a meeting.

It was at the colonial fairs that horse racing was one of the most conspicuous incidents. These fairs were held in all the colonies outside of New England, and even there they were occasionally held, except in Connecticut, where, as the unvera-cious Samuel Peters says, dancing, fishing, hunt-ing, skating, and sleighing on the ice were the only amusements allowed. Though the fairs were in most cases ordained by law, they were sometimes purely private undertakings, as that held at Rye, New Hampshire, which was promoted by an inn-keeper, or that at Williamsburg, in 1739, which found its support in a fund raised by a group of gentlemen.

The object of the fair was to bring people to-gether, to encourage trade, and "to provide a general commerce or traffic among persons that want to buy or sell either the product or manu-facture of the country or any other sorts of goods or merchandize." In some colonies the fairs, which usually lasted for three days, were held but once a year in the autumn but in others twice a year, in May and in September or October. On these occasions horses, oxen, cows, sheep, hogs, and sundry sorts of goods were exposed for sale. The people indulged in such varieties of sport as a slow horse race with a silver watch to the hindmost, a foot race at Williamsburg from the college to the capitol, a race for women, on Long Island, with a Holland smock and a chintz gown for prizes, a race by men in bags, and an obstacle race for boys. There were cudgeling bouts, bear baiting, gouging, a notoriously cruel sport, and catching a goose at full speed or a pig with a greased tail. There were also such other amusing entertainments as grinning contests by half a dozen men or women for a roll of tobacco or a plum pudding, and whistling contests for a guinea, in which the participants were to whistle selected tunes as clearly as possible without laughing. The people enjoyed puppet shows, ropewalking, and fortune telling; and the ubiquitous medicine hawker sold his wares from a stage "and by his harangues, the odd tricks of his Merry Andrew, and the surprising feats of his little boy" always attracted a crowd. The fairs were also utilized in Virginia as an occasion for paying debts, trading horses, buying land, and obtaining bills of exchange.

Prominent among more aristocratic colonial diversions were the balls and assemblies given in private and public houses, where dancing was the order of the evening. Dancing, though not strictly forbidden in New England, was not encouraged, particularly if it were promiscuous or mixed. Yet so frequent were the occasions for dancing that many dancing schools were conducted in the larger towns. One of the most noted was that of Charles Pelham in Boston, where in 1754 lessons were given three afternoons a week. State balls, governor's assemblies, and private gatherings were marked by lavish display, formal etiquette, and prolonged dancing, drinking, and card playing. The quality, who arrived in coaches, wore their most resplendent costumes, went through the steps of the stately minuet, and also joined in the jigs, reels, marches, country dances, and hornpipes which were all in vogue at that time.

Music, which was a popular colonial accomplishment, was taught as an important subject in a number of schools, and many a daughter was kept at her scales until she cried from sheer exhaustion. In the South the colonists were familiar with such musical instruments as the spinnet, harpsichord, pianoforte, viol, violin, violoncello, guitar, German flute, French horn, and jew's-harp. Thomas Jefferson was "vastly pleased" with Jenny Taliaferro's playing on the spinnet and singing. Benjamin Carter, son of Councilman Carter of Nomini Hall, had a guitar, a harpsichord, a pianoforte, a harmonica, a violin, a German flute, and an organ. He also had a good ear for music and, as Fithian tells us, was indefatigable in practice. Captain Goelet went to a "consort" in Boston, where the performers, playing on four small violins, one bass violin, a German flute, and an "indifrent small organ," did "as well as could be expected." Josiah Quincy attended a meeting of the St. Cecilia Society in Charleston in a "large inelegant building," where the performers were all at one end of the hall, and the music, he thought, "was good," the playing on the bass viols and French horns being "grand," but that on the harpsichord "badly done," though the performance of a recently arrived French violinist was "incomparable." "The capital defect of this concert," he said, "was want of an organ."

Interest in the drama in these early days was much less general than the love of music, owing to the rare opportunities which the people had for seeing plays. While there may have been private performances given by amateurs in the seventeenth century, the earliest of which we have any record were those given before Governor Spotswood in Williamsburg, probably in the theater erected in 1716, that in the "playhouse" in New York before 1733, and that in the court room in Charleston in 1735. Taverns, court rooms, and warehouses were used for much of the early acting, and the first theaters in Williamsburg, New York, Charleston, Philadelphia, and Annapolis, were crude affairs, rough unadorned buildings very much like warehouses or tobacco barns in appearance. There were no professional companies until 1750, when Murray, Kean, Lewis Hallam, and David Douglas began the history of the theater in America and aroused a great deal of interest in plays and playgoing from New York to Savannah. Nearly all the plays, both tragedies and comedies, of these days were of English origin. Some of these early dramas were *The Recruiting Officer*, *The Orphan*, *The Spanish Friar or the Double Discovery*, *The Jealous Wife*, *Theodosius or the Mourning Bride*, *The Distressed Mother*, *Love in a Village*, *The Provoked Husband*, *The School for Lovers*, and a few of

Shakespeare's plays, such as *The Tempest*, *King Lear*, *Hamlet*, and *Romeo and Juliet*. Though earlier plays had been written in America but not acted, there was performed at Philadelphia in 1767 the first American tragedy, *The Prince of Parthia*, by Thomas Godfrey, son of the William Godfrey, with whom Franklin boarded for a time, and who shares with Hadley the honor of inventing the quadrant. Though there was no theater in New England until later, in 1732, the New England *Weekly Journal* of Boston, in defiance of Puritan prejudice, printed in its columns a play, *The London Merchant*. Though the Quaker opposition was not overcome until 1754 in Philadelphia, when Hallam went there with his company, the first permanent theater in America, the Southwark, was built in that city in 1766, and it was there a year later that Godfrey's tragedy was performed.

During the twenty years preceding the Revolution, theatergoing was a constant diversion among the better class in the Middle and Southern Colonies, and Mrs. Manigault of Charleston tells us in her diary that she went five times in one week. Colonel Jones wrote from Williamsburg in 1736: "You may tell Betty Pratt [his stepdaughter] there has been but two plays acted since she went, which is *Cato* by the young gentlemen of the college, as they call themselves, and the *Busybody* by the company on Wednesday night last and I believe there will be another to-night. They have been at a great loss for a fine lady, who I think is called Dorinda, but that difficulty is overcome by finding her, which was to be the greatest secret and as such 'tis said to be Miss Anderson that came to town with Mrs. Carter." William Allason, writing from Falmouth, Virginia, in 1771, said: "The best sett of players that ever performed in America are to open the theater in Fredericksburg on Tuesday next and continue for some weeks." Quincy saw Hallam in *The Padlock* and *The Gamester* in New York in 1773 and thought him indifferent in tragedy but better in comedy, while some of his company "acted superlatively."

Occasional amusements of a less formal or permanent nature existed in great variety. Itinerant performers passed up and down the colonies. Dugee, an artist on the slack wire, began his exhibitions in 1732 at Van Dernberg's Garden in New York. Mrs. Eleanor Harvey made quite a sensation as a fortune teller shortly before the Revolution. Exhibitions of dwarfs, electrical devices and displays, musical clocks, and Punch and Judy shows were common in most of the cities and larger towns. Waxworks were also very popular; and of these the most famous were those of Mrs. Wright, with the figures of Whitefield and John Dickinson, and groups illustrating the Return of the Prodigal Son. The beginnings of a menagerie and circus may be seen in the exhibition of a lion in the Jerseys, New York, and Connecticut in 1729, the horses that did tricks and the dogs that rode sitting up in the saddle, and the "shows" that occasionally came to New England towns. On important occasions fireworks, rockets, wheels, and candles were set off. Michel gives an entertaining account of a display at Williamsburg in 1702, at which a number of mishaps occurred. The show began with a "reversed rocket, which was to pass along a string to an arbor where prominent ladies were seated, but it got stuck half-way and exploded. Two stars [wheels] were to revolve through the fireworks, but they succeeded no better than with the rockets. In short, nothing was successful, the rockets also refused to fly up, but fell down archlike, so that it was not worth while seeing. Most of the people, however, had never seen such things and praised them highly."

The calendar days of St. Andrew, St. Patrick,

St. David, and St. George were celebrated in the South with drinking and speechmaking, and St. Tammany Day was observed in Philadelphia with music and feasting. Christmas week was a period of merrymaking not only in the South but also among the Anglicans in the North, where a Christmas service was always held in King's Chapel in Boston. In both sections of the country the occasion was marked by presents to members of the family and to friends and by "boxes" (a term familiar to the Southerners and still in use in England) to the servants and tradesmen. It was customary to observe Gunpowder Day, the 5th of November, in Northern cities, where it was called Pope Day and was celebrated by boys and young men, who carried about in procession effigies of the Pope, the devil, and any one else who was for the moment in popular disfavor. The day, however, was accompanied by so much rowdiness and disturbance of the peace in Portsmouth, New Hampshire, that its continuance was forbidden in 1768 by order of the Assembly. Thanksgiving Day, that time-honored New England institution which originated with the Pilgrim Fathers in 1621, had become in the eighteenth century an annual November observance, proclaimed by the Governor. During this

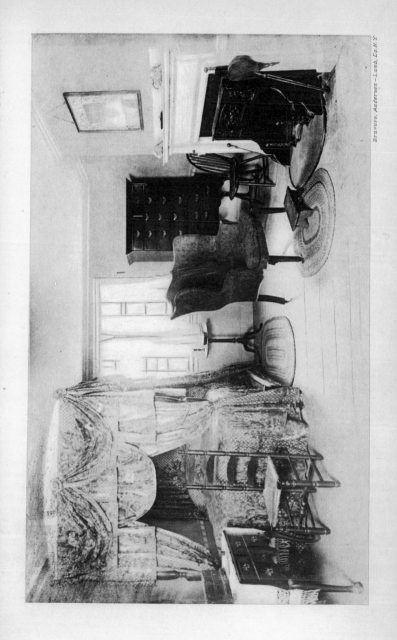

for every one was made in New England, at least
in Massachusetts and Connecticut, including the
former colonies of Plymouth and New Haven.
Here the colonists recognized the obligation of
teaching all children something and imposed on
the parents or the towns the duty of providing
local schools for the benefit of the community.
This obligation was so well understood that in laying out new towns, particularly after 1715, tracts
were frequently set aside for schools, not only in
Connecticut and Massachusetts but also in New
Hampshire, Maine, and the Connecticut settlement in the Wyoming Valley. The higher education necessary for preparing boys for college was
furnished partly by the grammar schools and
partly, perhaps to a larger extent in the earlier
period than afterwards, by ministers who conducted schools in their parsonages or rectories in
order to eke out their modest salaries.

The subjects taught in the log or clapboarded
schoolhouses were reading, writing, arithmetic,
and the catechism. Spelling was introduced early,
with little effect, however, as far as uniformity was
concerned; but English grammar was not cultivated in the schools even in the larger centers
until about 1760. The first aids to learning were

the hornbook, the A B C book, and the primer. Dilworth's speller was in general use, if we may judge from its frequent appearance in the lists of books imported. Governor Wolcott of Connecticut tells us that he never went to school a day in his life, but was taught by his mother at home, and that he did not learn to read and write until he was eleven years old; and his case was probably by no means exceptional. Men in their wills often made provision for the education of their children, but in most cases they desired nothing more than reading and good penmanship; and an apprentice who had been taught to write "a legiable joyning hand playne to be read" was deemed properly treated by his master. Grammar schools where Latin and Greek were taught were rare. The Hopkins Grammar Schools in Hartford and New Haven and the Boston Latin School are noteworthy examples of higher education in New England, but even these schools did not reach a very high level.

Outside of New England, Maryland was the only colony which had a rudimentary system of public education, for under the Free School Act of 1694 a series of schools supported by the counties was planned, to be free for all or at least a number of the pupils attending. Such schools were started

sometimes by persons of wealth who would sub-
scribe what was needed; sometimes they were endowed by a single benefactor who would give
money for this purpose during his lifetime or by
will at his death. The original purpose of the free
school was to provide an education for those who
were unable to pay tuition. Even in New England,
tuition was usually charged in most of the town
schools, particularly of Massachusetts, during the
seventeenth century and the first quarter of the
eighteenth. After this time, however, the maintenance of schools by general taxation became
more frequent.

How many such schools were established in
Maryland it is difficult to say. Though an effort
was made in 1696 to erect a school under the terms
of the Free School Act, nothing was accomplished
at the time, and as late as 1707 Governor Seymour
could say that not one step had been taken for the
encouragement of learning in Maryland. The fact
however that the school founded at Annapolis was
called King William's School confirms the belief
that a building was erected in 1701, before the
King's death, though it is not unlikely that little
or no progress was made during the first few years
of its existence. To this school, which was destined

in time to grow into St. John's College, Benjamin
Leonard Calvert left a legacy in 1733, and from
that date, under the impetus of masters and ushers
obtained from England, its career was prosperous
and continuous. On the other side of the Bay,
in Queen Anne County, a second school was established in 1723. From the records, which are
still extant, we learn that the subjects taught
were reading, writing, arithmetic, English, surveying, navigation, and geography, and that the
school possessed a fine assortment of globes,
maps, and charts. It offered an extensive course
in mathematics, in which it made use of a
quadrant, scales, and compasses, and many English textbooks. For a colonial school its collection of Latin and Greek texts, treatises, and
lexicons was unusually complete. But despite
its equipment and the fact that in plan and
outfit it was manifestly ahead of its time, the
school had a checkered career and a hard strug-
gle for existence.

Among both the Quakers and the Germans
education was intimately bound up with religion
and church organization. The Friends' Public
School, founded at Philadelphia in 1689 and destined to become the Penn Charter School of today,

was not characteristic of the educational life of Pennsylvania. Wherever they lived, the Quakers and Germans tried to establish schools which were more or less under the supervision of their churches and hence lay outside the movement which led to the founding of the public school system in America. Though there were in Pennsylvania many private schools, it cannot be said that this colony was abreast educationally of either New England or Virginia. The Dutch in New York likewise established a system of parochial schools, of which there were two in the period from 1751 to 1762 in the city itself. But by far the most elaborate effort to build up schools in the interest of a particular form of doctrine and worship was that made by the Society for the Propagation of the Gospel in Foreign Parts, which, after its foundation in 1701, entered upon a vast scheme of evangelization in all the colonies, including the West Indies. The establishment of libraries and schools formed a most important part of this undertaking. In New York alone, where the plan found its most complete application, between five and ten elementary schools were started. A single "charity" or free school in the city, which pay pupils also attended, was inaugurated in 1710 and, under such deserving schoolmasters as the Huddlestons and Joseph Hildreth, ran a continuous course until the Revolution. Though the subjects taught were mainly the three R's, the Psalms, Catechism, Bible, and church doctrine, it has been justly said that "the patronage of schools in America by this Society formed the foremost philanthropic movement in education during the colonial period."

In the colonies of New Jersey, Virginia, North and South Carolina, and Georgia, and to some extent in Maryland and New York also, the system of education in vogue was a combination of private tutors, small pay schools, and an occasional endowed free school or academy. The tutorial method and the sending of children to England for their education were possible only among the wealthier families, and as free schools were not numerous in these colonies, it follows that public education there was not furnished to the children at large. Perth Amboy, for instance, seems to have had no school at all until 1773, and though the Society for the Propagation of the Gospel sent schoolmasters to Burlington, the results were meager, and New Jersey remained during colonial times without an educational system apart from the usual catechizing in the churches.

In Virginia education was largely a private business, for though the Syms and Eaton free schools,
the oldest institutions of the kind in the colonies,
continued to exist, they did not grow either in
wealth or in efficiency. Virginia had many private schools, such as that at St. Mary's in Caroline
County, kept by Jonathan Boucher, who, in addition to his duties as rector, took boys at twenty
pounds for board and education, or that of William
Prentis in Williamsburg, who, though a clerk at
the time and afterwards a merchant, had a school
where he taught Latin and Greek and took tuition fees. Prentis's pupils read Ovid, Cato, Quin-
tus Curtius, Terence, Justin, Phædrus, Virgil, and
Cæsar, and used a "gradus," a "pantheon," a
"vocabulary," a Greek grammar, and two dic-
tionaries. Sometimes the parents would advertise
for "any sober diligent person qualified to keep a
country school," guaranteeing a certain number
of pupils. That the results were not always satisfactory, even among the best families, is apparent
from Nathaniel Burwell's unfraternal characteri-
zation of his brother Lewis as one who could neither
read, spell, nor cipher correctly, and was in "no
ways capable of managing his own affairs or fit for
any gentleman's conversation."

Prominent planters obtained tutors from England, Scotland, and the Northern Colonies, and the accounts given by some of these teachers — Benjamin Harrower at Captain Daingerfield's, Philip Fithian at Councilman Carter's, and the Reverend Jonathan Boucher at Captain Dixon's — throw light on the conditions attending the education of a planter's children. The conditions thus described were probably more agreeable than was elsewhere the case, for in other instances not only were tutors indentured servants but frequently were treated as such and made to feel the inferiority of their position. One John Warden refused to accept the post of tutor in a Virginia family, unless the planter and his wife and children would treat him "as a gentleman." The following letter from a Virginian to Micajah Perry of London in 1741 must be similar to many dispatched for a like purpose: "If possible I desire you will send me by Wilcox a schoolmaster to teach my children to read and write and cypher [the children were two girls, sixteen and twelve, and a boy five years old]. I would willingly have such a person as Mr. Lock describes, but cant expect such on such wages as I can afford, but I desire he may be a modest, sober, discreet person. His wages I leave to your discretion, the usual wages here for a Latin master from Scotland is £20 a year, but they commonly teach the children the Scotch dialect which they never can wear off." In addition to his employer's children the tutor was generally allowed to take other pupils for whom he could charge tuition. Harrower did this but had considerable trouble collecting the fees, and John Portress kept a school on Gibbons's plantation in Georgia where he taught the neighboring children writing, grammar, and "practical" mathematics. In some instances the tutor acted also as a general factotum for the planter, even serving as overseer or steward. James Ellerton, the English tutor on Madam Smith's estate in South Carolina, had as much to do with corn, pigs, and fences as he did with reading and the rule of three.

A great many New York, Maryland, Virginia, and South Carolina boys of the more wealthy families were sent abroad for their education. The sons of Oliver De Lancey of New York went to England, those of William Byrd, 3d, were at Sinnock's in Kent in 1767, Alexander and John Spotswood remained at Eton four years, and Samuel Swann of North Carolina studied in England in 1758. Keith William Pratt, Thomas Jones's stepson, at the age of fourteen was at Dr.

L'Herundell's school in Chelsea, learning French, Latin, Greek, writing, arithmetic, drawing, and fencing "as far as it is thought necessary for a gentleman." His sister Betty, aged nine, wrote him from Virginia, when he was eight years old: "You are got as far as the rule of three in arithmetic, but I cant cast up a sum in addition cleverly, but I am striving to do better every day. I can perform a great many dances and am now learning the Sibell, but I cannot speak a word of French."

Despite their English education, few Southern boys were as precocious as Jonathan Edwards, who began Latin at six, was reading Locke *On the Human Understanding* when other boys were lost in *Robinson Crusoe*,[1] and was ready for college at thirteen; or as Samuel Johnson, later president of King's College, who was ambitious to learn Hebrew at six, complained of his tutor as "such a wretched poor scholar" at ten, entered Yale at fourteen, and capped the climax of a long and erudite career by publishing a Hebrew and English grammar at the age of seventy-one. Few could quote classical writers or show such wide reading and extensive

[1] Perhaps it is only fair to note that at a later date John C. Calhoun was reading Locke at the age of thirteen. But he was not a tidewater Southerner and furthermore was educated at Yale.

knowledge of books as did Cotton Mather or
Thomas Hutchinson, but few in the South were
surpassed by the boys in the North in versatility
and knowledge of the world. Many Southern lads
went to the Northern colleges at Philadelphia,
Princeton, and New Haven, and a few to Northern schools to study some such special subject
as navigation.

In the Carolinas there were fewer tutors than
in Virginia. A large number of private schools,
however, was maintained in Wilmington, Charleston, and Savannah. There was a provincial free
school in Charleston and another at Childesbury
in the same colony, but the free school founded by
Colonel James Inness "for the benefit of the youth
of North Carolina" was not started in Wilmington
until 1783. South of Williamsburg there was no
"seminary for academical studies," says Whitefield,
who tried to turn his Orphan House in Savannah
into a college in 1764. The private schools which
predominated were promoted by private persons
who advertised their wares and offered a varied
assortment of educational attractions such as arithmetic, algebra, geometry, trigonometry, surveying, dialing, navigation, gauging, and fortifica-
tion, but there is reason to believe that the results

which they obtained did not justify the claims of the schoolmasters. Some, from motives in which desire for a living was probably a larger factor than zeal for education, announced that they were ready "to go out, to receive day pupils, or to take boarders."

In the mercantile centers the desire for a practical education was always strong. As early as 1713 in New York a demand arose for courses in navigation, surveying, mensuration, astronomy, and "merchants' accounts." In 1755 a master by the name of James Bragg offered to teach navigation to "gentlemen Sailors and others . . . in a short time and reasonable." In Charleston, George Austin, Henry Laurens's partner, voiced a general feeling and forecast a modern controversy when he deemed training in business more to his son's advantage "than to pore over Latin and Greek authors of little utility to a young man intended for a mercantile career." Here and there throughout the colonies there were evening schools, as in New York, Charleston, and Savannah; French schools, as in New York and New Rochelle; besides schools for dancing, music, and fencing, and at least one school for teaching "the art of manly defense." Whether shorthand was anywhere taught is doubtful and highly improbable, yet from Henry Wolcott, Jr., of Windsor and Roger Williams of Rhode Island to Jonathan Boucher of Virginia and Maryland there were those who were familiar with it, and occasional references to writings in "characters" would point in the same direction.

As far as girls were concerned, the opportunities for education were limited. As a rule they were not admitted to the public schools of New England, and coeducation prevailed apparently only in some of the private schools, the Venerable Society's Charity School in New York, and in Pennsylvania, particularly among the Germans. In 1730 the Charity School had sixty-eight pupils, twenty of whom were girls. The Moravian girls' schools at Bethlehem, Pennsylvania, and Salem, North Carolina, were unique of their kind. Day schools for young ladies were subsequently opened by men and women everywhere for the teaching of reading, writing, "flourishing," ciphering, French, English, and literature, and for instruction in embroidery, the making of coats of arms, painting, "Dresden, Catgut, and all sorts of colored work" and various other feminine accomplishments of the day deemed "necessary," as one prospectus puts it, "to the amusement of persons of fortune who have taste."

A boarding school for girls was opened at Norfolk, Virginia, and another in Charleston, to the latter of which Laurens sent his eldest daughter; but boarding schools, though not uncommon for boys, particularly after 1750, were rare for colonial maidens, some of whom from the South were sent abroad, while many others were taught at home. Manuals on home training were known and used, one of which, *The Mother's Advice to her Daughters*, described as "a small treatise on the education of ladies," was imported into New England in 1766.

Many efforts were made to instruct and Christianize both Indians and negroes. Among the best-known of these are the labors of Jonathan Edwards among the Indians at Stockbridge, of David and John Brainard among those of New York, New Jersey, and Pennsylvania, and of Eleazer Wheelock and his missionaries among the Oneidas and Tuscaroras and at the Indian school in Lebanon. There was also an Indian school connected with William and Mary College; and Massachusetts in 1751 proposed to start two schools for the instruction of negro boys and girls, to be boarded and taught at the expense of the colony. The Society for the Propagation of the Gospel made this work

a very important part of its program and instructed
its missionaries and schoolmasters "to be ready,
as they have opportunity, to teach and instruct the
Indians and Negroes and their children." As a
consequence schools for this purpose were opened
in many colonial towns and parishes. The pioneer,
Dr. McSparran, gave much of his time to catechizing and teaching both Indians and Negroes, and
there must have been others of the clergy doing the
same unselfish work. Even Harrower, the Virginia
tutor already mentioned, read and taught the
catechism to a "small congregation of negroes" on
Captain Daingerfield's plantation. One of the
most famous efforts of missionary education was
that of Commissary Garden of South Carolina, who
started a negro school in Charleston in 1744, to
which "all the negro and Indian children of the
parish" were to go for instruction "without any
charge to their masters." Funds were collected,
a building was erected, and the school continued
for twenty-two years with from thirty to seventy
children, who were taught reading, spelling, and
the chief principles of the Christian religion.

In the realm of the higher education, three
colleges, Harvard, William and Mary, and Yale,
were already prominent colonial institutions, but

Princeton in 1753 was still "our little infant college of New Jersey," and the College of Rhode Island (now Brown University), and Dartmouth, the outgrowth of Wheelock's work at Lebanon, were hardly as yet fairly on their feet. King's College (now Columbia University) and the College and Academy of Philadelphia (now University of Pennsylvania), organized to promote more liberal and practical studies, were just entering on their great careers. The degrees granted by the colleges were Bachelor of Arts and honorary Master of Arts, to which in some instances Bachelors of Arts of other colleges were admitted. Higher degrees, such as Doctor of Divinity, Doctor of Laws, and Doctor of Civil Law, were not conferred by American colleges but were granted to many a colonist, chiefly among the clergy, by Oxford, Cambridge, Aberdeen, Glasgow, and, highest in repute, by Edinburgh. Occasionally a colonist received a degree from a continental university such as Padua or Utrecht. Though the cost of a degree in those days ran as high as twenty-five pounds, there was considerable competition among the New England clergy to obtain this distinction and not a little wirepulling was involved in the process.

For professional training in medicine, surgery,

law, and art, many colonists went abroad to England, Scotland, and the Continent, where they
studied anatomy, surgery, medicine, pharmacy,
and chemistry, read law at one or other of the Inns
of Court in London, or traveled, as did Benjamin
West and John Singleton Copley, to see the leading
galleries of Europe. One of the first to study surgery abroad was Thomas Bulfinch of Boston, who
was in Paris in 1720 studying obstetrics. He declared in his letters that few surgeons in America
knew much of the business and that there was no
place in the world like Paris. "I am studying," he
writes, "with the greatest man midwife in Paris
(and I might say in the universe for that business)."
In 1751 his son Thomas also went over to study
pharmacy and boarded in London at the "chym-
ists where drugs and medicines were prepared for
the hospitals." Later he turned to surgery, rose
at seven, as he wrote his father, walked to Great
Marlboro Street, Soho, three miles away from his
lodgings in Friday Street, St. Paul's, where, "I am
busied in dissection of dead bodies to four in the
afternoon, and often times don't allow myself time
to dine. At six I go to Mr. Hunter's lecture [in
anatomy], where I am kept till nine." He tells us
that he did chemical experiments in his chamber

and diverted himself by seeing Garrick act. But the majority of colonial doctors who studied abroad went to Edinburgh. Dr. Walter Jones of Virginia, one of the most distinguished of them, took his degree there in 1769, and has left us in his letters a delightful account of his sojourn in that city.

The colonists spoke a variety of languages. There were thousands who could not write or speak English, particularly among those who, like the Germans, came from foreign lands and not only retained but taught their native tongue in America. The Celtic Highlanders who settled at Cross Creek wrote and spoke Gaelic, and specimens of their letters and accounts still survive. Dutch continued to be spoken in New York, and in Albany and its neighborhood it was the prevailing tongue in colonial times and even long after the colonial period had come to an end. Many of the New York merchants were bilinguists, and some of them — Robert Sanders, for example, — wrote readily in English, Dutch, and French. The Huguenots adapted themselves to the use of English more easily than did the Germans and Dutch, though many of them in New York and South Carolina continued to use French, with the result that even their negroes acquired a kind of French lingo. The advantage of knowing French was generally recognized and among those who regretted their inability to speak the language was Cuyler of New York. A knowledge of French was desired partly as an accomplishment and partly as a business asset, for those who, like Charles Carroll, had been educated in France thus had a distinct advantage over their fellows.

Other languages were less generally understood. Moses Lindo, the indigo inspector of Charleston, was one of those who spoke Spanish, and many of the Jewish merchants and some of the foreign indentured servants were familiar with both Spanish and Portuguese. There must have been interpreters of Spanish in Connecticut in 1752 when there was some trouble over a Spanish ship at New London, for much of the evidence is in Spanish, and Governor Wolcott, who knew nothing of the language, had the documents translated for him. To a greater extent even than today, the exigencies of commerce demanded of those trading with France, Holland, Spain, Portugal, and the West Indies a knowledge of the languages used in those countries. Many colonists who went as merchants or factors to Amsterdam, Bordeaux, Lisbon, or the towns of the foreign West Indies, became proficient in one or more tongues. In all the colonies there were agents and missionaries who were familiar with Indian speech. In addition to such professionals as Conrad Weiser, Daniel Claus, Peter Wraxall, and Wheelock's missionaries, there were others who, though less regularly employed, acquired in one way or another a knowledge of Indian speech and were able to act as interpreters. Many of the slaves were African Negroes who spoke no English at all or only what was called "Black English," and for that reason among others the Negro born in America always commanded a higher price in the market. Among the indentured servants were large numbers of Welsh who spoke only Gaelic, of English who spoke only their Cornish, Somersetshire, Lancashire, or Yorkshire dialect, and of Irish who spoke "with the brogue very much on their tongues."

Not only were there thousands of men and women in the colonies who could hardly read and who could only make their mark, but there were also thousands who had little or no interest in reading or in collecting books. The smaller farmers and planters, artisans and laborers, confined their reading to the Bible or New Testament, the psalter or hymn book, and an occasional religious work such as the *Practice of Piety* or *Pilgrim's Progress*. Printed sermons also were popular, particularly after 1740, when those of Whitefield began to be circulated.   Among the volumes with which the colonial reader was familiar were the almanacs — the *Farmer's Almanac* of Whittemore or Nathaniel Ames in Massachusetts, Wells's *Register and Almanac*, the *Hochdeutsche-Amerikanische Kalender*, Tobler's *South Carolina and Georgia Almanac*, and scores of others.   From these the colonists obtained all the scientific knowledge they possessed of sun, moon, tides, and weather predictions, as well as a great variety of religious, political, and miscellaneous information, a diverting assortment of jokes, puzzles, and charades for idle hours, and tables of exchanges, interest, and money values for the man of business.   Except the Bible, probably no book was held in greater esteem or was more widely read in the colonies in the eighteenth century than the almanac.   In various forms and from the hands of many publishers it circulated from coast to back country and from Maine to Georgia and was the colonists' *vade mecum* of knowledge.   It was even more popular than the newspaper, which, though issued at this time in all the colonies except New Jersey, was expensive, difficult to distribute, and very limited in circulation.

Collections of books, other than those on the shelves of the libraries and in the stocks of the booksellers, were largely confined to the houses of ministers, lawyers, doctors, wealthy merchants, and planters. Early libraries, such as those of John Goodburne in Virginia (1635), William Brewster in Plymouth (1644), and Samuel Eaton in New Haven (1656), were brought from England and consisted chiefly of theological works, with a sprinkling of classical authors and a few books on mathematics and geography. None of these collections contained works of fiction. William Brewster had a volume or two of poetry and history. The library of William FitzHugh of Virginia (1671) included books on history, law, medicine, physics, and morals, but nothing of literature, essays, poetry, or romance. The law library of Arthur Spicer of Virginia (1701) was remarkable for its scope and variety; and the briefs of his contemporaries, William Pitkin and Richard Edwards of Connecticut, show that they too must have had the use of the leading law books of the day. Cotton Mather's library began when the owner was but nineteen with ninety-six volumes, of which eighty-one were theological and the remainder works on history, philosophy, and philology. The seventeenth century, both in England and America, was manifestly an age of heavy literature.

With the reigns of Anne and the Georges, a new literary activity began to make itself felt. Localities occupied by Quakers, Moravians, Wesleyans, and Covenanters disclose large numbers of books of denominational piety, many of them in Dutch, German, and Gaelic. Among those in English were Ellwood's *Life*, Penn's *No Cross, No Crown*, Elias Hook's *Spirits of the Martyrs Revived*, Sewall's *History*, Barclay's *Apology*, Fox's *Journal*, and Boston's *Fourfold State*. The increased interest in agriculture, commerce, law, government, and housekeeping led the colonists to read books of a practical nature such as *The Art of Cooking*, *The Complete Housewife*, Miller's *Gardener's Dictionary*, Longley's *Book of Gardening*, Burrough's *Navigation Book*, Leadbetter's *Dialling*, Wright's *Negotiator*, Mathew's *Concerning Computation of Time*, Mair's *Bookkeeping*, and other brochures relating to commerce, as well as many works, too numerous to be cited here, on law, local government, the practice of medicine, anatomy, surgery, surveying, and navigation. There were also many editions

of the British statutes, law reports, proceedings of
Parliament, and treatises on admiralty and marine
matters, all of which were imported. Many of the
leading men, particularly in the South, subscribed
regularly to the *London Magazine*, the *Gentleman's
Magazine*, Rider's *Almanac*, Eachard's *Gazetteer*,
the *Court Calendar*, and other British periodical
publications.

There was a close literary relation maintained
between England and the colonies, and newspapers,
books, and magazines were constantly sent by
merchants across the Atlantic to their correspondents in America. An ever widening interest in
public affairs was bringing in a steadily increasing number of histories, biographies, voyages, and
travels — such as the histories of Rapin, Robert-
son, Mosheim, Raleigh, Clarendon, Burnet, Hume,
Voltaire, and Salmon; the lives of Julius Cæsar,
Oliver Cromwell, Louis XII, Marlborough, and
Eugene of Savoy; and the voyages of Churchill and
Anson. As time went on, an improving taste on
the part of the colonists for poetry, essays, and
fiction, and translations from the classics and foreign languages began to show itself. Among the
chief poets were Chaucer, Milton, Dryden, and
Pope, as well as such minor men as Gower, Butler,

Donne, Waller, Herbert, Cowley, Congreve, and Prior. Among the essays popular in the colonies were those of Montaigne, Bacon, Swift, and Bolingbroke, as well as the contributions of Steele and Addison to the *Tatler* and the *Spectator* and of Johnson to the *Rambler*. In fiction we find the writings of Richardson, Fielding, Sterne, Goldsmith, and Aphra Behn, and the romances, *The Turkish Spy*, *The London Spy*, and *The Jewish Spy;* and in the drama the works of Ben Jonson, Shakespeare, and Dryden. Among the translations from other languages were the *Iliad* and the *Odyssey*, Cervantes's *Don Quixote*, Lesage's *Gil Blas* and *Le Diable Boiteux*, Montesquieu's *Lettres persanes*, and the *Mémoires* of Cardinal de Retz, which was amazingly popular. For young people there were *Gulliver's Travels*, *Robinson Crusoe*, *The Arabian Nights*, and a great abundance of fables, gift books, and short histories.

As an indication of the range and variety of these colonial collections of books it is interesting to note that here and there were to be found such works as Hoyle's *Games*, *Memoirs of Gamesters*, Madox on the *Exchequer*, Harrington's *Oceana*, and even More's *Utopia*. As for law books, Robert Bell, the publisher of Philadelphia, imported in

1771 a thousand sets of the English edition of Blackstone's *Commentaries*, and himself issued a thousand sets more in four royal octavo volumes, which he sold by subscription. Henceforth we begin to find, for the first time, copies of Blackstone appearing in colonial libraries and inventories. In many of the private libraries were works in French, but rarely in other languages except among the Germans. Grey Elliott, an English official in Savannah, was apparently an exception, for he had two hundred volumes "in several languages," but what these languages were we do not know. In all libraries were to be found works issued from the various presses in America. The books of Councilman Carter of Nomini Hall numbered 1503 volumes, and those of William Byrd, 3d, of which there were more than four thousand in many languages, constituted what was probably at that time the largest private library in America.

The practice of lending books was bound to be common in a country where they were rare and expensive and where neighborliness was a virtue. A number of lists which are in existence show the prevalence of the custom. The catalogue of the library of Godfrey Pole of Virginia (1716), containing 115 titles, shows that about thirty books were out on loan and that several others had been lent and returned.   In colonial correspondence we come upon such notes as this from a Dr. Farquharson of Charleston to Peter Manigault in 1756, in which he says that he is sending back "the books and magazines and would be obliged for a reading of Mr. Pope's works."

From lending books as a personal favor it was but a short step to the establishment of private circulating libraries. As early as the beginning of the eighteenth century the Reverend Thomas Bray, commissary of Maryland, had begun his series of "lending libraries" in "the Market Towns" for "any of the clergy to have recourse to or to borrow books out of, as there shall be occasion."   How many such lending libraries were actually established it is difficult to say, but there was one at Bath, North Carolina, and another at Annapolis.   There appear to have been, particularly in the South, other collections quasi public in character, such as the private library of Edward Moseley of Edenton, which was thrown open for public use. These libraries differed from the circulating libraries of such booksellers as Garret Noël of New York and John Mein of Boston, for example, in that no charge was made for the privilege of borrowing.

Perhaps the first library that may in a sense be called public was that owned by the town of Boston and kept in the "library room" of the Town House. It was started in 1656 and came to an untimely end in the fire of 1747. While it may have been accessible to readers, it was in no sense a lending library, for its massive folios and their equally ponderous contents must have made little appeal to any but the clergy. Much more important as an aid to the spread of good literature were the subscription libraries which came into existence as soon as books were made less bulky and more interesting and entertaining. Before the middle of the eighteenth century associations began to be formed for the buying and lending of books. Of these the most famous was the Library Association of Philadelphia, founded in 1731 by a group of fifty persons, headed by Franklin, which ten years later published its first real catalogue. The Pomfret Association of Connecticut was established in 1740, that of Charleston in 1748, and that of Lancaster in 1759. To the last named Governor Hamilton and many leading Pennsylvanians gave money, globes, and astronomical apparatus.

Other instances of the spread of this movement were the Georgia Library, started in 1763, and the Social Library at Salem, Massachusetts, established some time before the Revolution. But there was at that time in the colonies no library supported by public funds and similar to the free public libraries of today.

The bookseller was an important colonial character. Though many of the colonists imported their own books directly from England, by far the larger number obtained what they wanted from those who made bookselling a trade. Merchants and storekeepers in all the large towns and along the Maryland and Virginia rivers carried in stock books which they obtained from England and Scotland. The inventories and invoices of these dealers are always interesting as showing their estimate of the popular taste. Though John Usher of Boston and Portsmouth was merchant and bookseller combined, few of the merchants did more than carry a small stock of books for sale, while on the other hand scarcely any of the booksellers concerned themselves with trade. They imported and sold books, published books and pamphlets, bound books, did job printing of all kinds, including blank forms for bonds, certificates, mortgages, and charter parties. They also made up and issued the newspapers of the day, served generally as public printers for their colonies, acted as postmasters in many towns, kept inquiry bureaus and intelligence offices for their localities, and were a local source of information. They also sold pens, ink, stationery, and all sorts of school necessities. The scope of their activities was perhaps less varied in the North than in the South, but everywhere they were indispensable in the life of their neighborhood. So important did these men become in colonial life that when Boston suffered heavily by the great fire of 1711 her most serious loss was the destruction of nearly all her bookselling establishments.

CHAPTER VII

THE CURE OF SOULS

THERE were many religious denominations in America in the eighteenth century. The Congregationalists predominated in New England, but outside of that region they found little support. The Church of England was dominant in the South and by 1750 had established itself in every colony from New Hampshire to Georgia. This growth was due in part to the fact that most of the Huguenots and many of the Lutherans went over to Anglicanism, but also in largest measure to the activities of the Society for the Propagation of the Gospel in Foreign Parts, generally known as the "S. P. G." but frequently called the "Venerable Society."

The Dutch in their Reformed Church constituted the oldest body of Calvinists in America. The Germans — some of them also Calvinists in their own Reformed Church — were in many cases

Lutherans or Moravians, chiefly in New York, Pennsylvania, and North Carolina, and in other cases were tinctured with pietism and mysticism. The Scotch-Irish were of a sterner religious temper than any of these and, tracing their spiritual ancestry back to the Presbyterianism of Scotland and the north of Ireland, they looked upon their religion as a subject worthy of constant thought and frequent discussion.

Among the denominations associated with no particular race or locality, the Baptists were nevertheless most strongly entrenched in Rhode Island, with a somewhat precarious hold on other parts of New England and on South Carolina. The Friends or Quakers, finding their earliest home also in Rhode Island, became specially prominent in the Middle Colonies, Virginia, and North Carolina, where their meetinghouses were often "in lonesome places in the woods." The Methodists, at this time with no thought of becoming a separate denomination, began their career as a spiritual force in America with Robert Strawbridge in western Maryland about 1764. Most of the Roman Catholics were to be found in Maryland and a few in other colonies; the Jews had synagogues in Newport, New York, Philadelphia, and Charleston;

but there was no separate African church until the first was set up in Williamsburg in 1791.

Of all these denominations the most powerful and influential were the Congregational and the Anglican, so that the meetinghouse in New England and the church in the Southern Colonies came to be distinctive and conspicuous features in the religious life of America. The meetinghouse, usually built of wood but toward the end of the period sometimes of brick, was situated in the center of the town. It was at first a plain, unadorned, rectangular structure, sometimes painted and sometimes not, without tower or steeple, and not unlike the Quaker meetinghouse and the Wesleyan chapel of a later day. Later buildings were constructed after English models, with the graceful spire characteristic of the work of Sir Christopher Wren, and represented a type to which the Presbyterian and Dutch Reformed churches tended to conform. At one end of the building rose the tower and spire, with a bell and a clock, if the congregation could afford them; at the other end or at the side was the porch. In addition to the pleasing proportions which the building as a whole showed, even the doors and windows manifested a certain striving for architectural beauty of a refined and rather severe kind. The interior was usually bare and unattractive; the pulpit stood on one side, high above the pews, and was made in the shape of an hourglass or with a curved front, and stood under a sounding board, which was introduced less perhaps for its acoustic value than to increase the dignity of the preacher. The body of the house was filled with high square pews, within which were movable seats capable of being turned back for the convenience of the worshipers, who always stood during the long prayers. The pews were the property of the occupiers, who viewed them as part of the family patrimony. Assignment of pews followed social rank; front seats were reserved for the deacons; convenient sittings were set apart for the deaf; the side seats were for those of lesser degree, and the gallery for the children. There were no free seats in colonial days, except for the very poor. In these meetinghouses there were neither fires nor lights, with the result that evening services could not be held. In the winter season the chill of the building must have wrought havoc upon tender physiques and imperiled the lives of those unlucky infants whose fate it was to be baptized with icy water.[1]

[1] "It was so cold a Lord's Day," says Checkley in his diary (Jan. 19, 1735), "that the water for Baptism was considerably frozen."

The journey to meeting was frequently an arduous undertaking for those living in the outlying parts of a township, as they sometimes were obliged to cross mountains and rivers in order to be present. From distant points the farmers drove to meeting, bringing their wives and children and prepared to spend the day. In summer they brought their own dinners with them; in winter they found refuge in the "Sabba' day" houses or were entertained at the fireside of friends who lived near the meetinghouse. The gathering of the townspeople at meeting was a social as well as a religious event, for friends had an opportunity for greeting each other, and the farmers exchanged news and talked crops during the noon hour, in the shade of the building, under the wagon sheds where the horses were tied, or sitting on the tombstones in the burying ground near by, while their wives and daughters gossiped in the porch or even in the pews, for in New England no one looked upon the meetinghouse as merely a sacred place. One of the earliest steps taken in the formation of a new town in New England was the erection of a separate meetinghouse for the members who lived too far away for convenient and regular attendance.

The minister was truly the leader of his people. He comforted and reproved them, guided their spiritual footsteps, advised them in matters domestic and civil, and gave unity to their ecclesiastical life. He was the chief citizen of the town, reverenced by the old and regarded with something akin to awe by the young. When a stranger asked Parson Phillips of the South Church at Andover if he were "the parson who serves here," he received the reply, "I am, Sir, the parson who rules here," and the external bearing of this colonial minister lent weight to his claim. It was the habit of Parson Phillips to walk with his household in a stately procession from the parsonage to the meetinghouse, with his wife on his right, his negro servant on his left, and his children following in the rear. When he entered the building, the congregation rose and stood until he had taken his place in the pulpit. Though he preached with an hourglass at his side, he never failed to run over the conventional sixty minutes. His sermons, like nearly all those preached in New England, were written out and read with solemnity and rarely with attempts at oratory. They were blunt and often terrifying; they laid down unpalatable ethical standards; they emphasized rigid theological doctrines; and in language which was plain, earnest, and uncompromising, they inveighed against such human weaknesses as swearing, drunkenness, fornication, and sleeping in church. Mather Byles of Boston, another colonial pastor, preached an hour and then turning over the hourglass said, "Now we will take a second glass." Sermons of two hours were not unknown, and there were those who "in one lazy tone, through the long, heavy, painful page" drawled on, making work for the tithingman, whose fur-tipped rod was often needed to waken the slumbering. The thrifty colonial preacher numbered his sermons, stored them away or bound them in volumes, and often repeated them many times.

The hardships of the New England minister were many. Jonathan Lee of Salisbury, Connecticut, occupied, until his log house was finished, a room temporarily fitted up at the end of a blacksmith's shop with stools for chairs and slabs for tables. He even had at times to carry his own corn to the mill to be ground. As country parishes were large and rambling and the congregation was widely scattered, the minister often preached in different sections and was obliged to ride many miles to visit and comfort his parishioners. His salary was small, fifty pounds and upwards, with more if he were married. Jonathan Edwards in 1744 wrote to his people in Northampton that he wanted a fixed salary and not one determined from year to year, as he had a growing family to provide for. Many a minister received a part of his stipend in provisions and firewood, and eked out his meager salary by earning a little money taking pupils. Yet in spite of these hardships men stayed long in the places to which they were called. Pastorates of sixty years are known; Eliphalet Williams of Glastonbury served fifty-five years, and his grandfather, father, and son each ministered half a century or longer. Three generations of Baptist clergymen in Groton served one church 125 years.

The New England ministers did not limit their preaching to the Sabbath day or their sermons to theological and ethical subjects. They officiated on many public occasions — at funerals, installations, and ordinations, on fast days, Thanksgiving days, and election days — and often forced the Governor and deputies to listen to a sermon two or three hours long. Many of these sermons were printed by the colony, by the church, by subscription, or in the case of funeral sermons by special provision in the will of the deceased. Parson

Phillips had twenty such sermons printed, and on the title-page of one dealing with some terrifying topic appears an ominous skull and crossbones. Funeral discourses and election sermons are among the commonest which have survived, but, taken as a whole, they are unfortunately among the least trustworthy of historical records.

The Anglican churches in the eighteenth century were generally built of brick but varied considerably in size, shape, and adornment. Except for a few — such as Trinity Church, Newport, which followed the Wren model, King's Chapel, Boston, which was of hewn stone, and McSparran's Narragansett church, which is described as a very dignified and elegant structure — the buildings of this denomination in New England were small and unpretentious and constructed of wood. In the South they were more stately and impressive in both external appearance and internal adornment. St. Mary's at Burlington, Christ Church and St. Peter's at Philadelphia, St. Anne's at Annapolis, Bruton Church at Williamsburg, St. Paul's at Edenton, and St. Philip's at Charleston were all noble structures, and there were many others of less repute which were examples of good architecture. Often these churches were surrounded by high brick walls and the interior was fitted with mahogany seats and stone-flagged aisles. Conspicuous were the altar and pulpit, both richly adorned, the canopied pew for the Governor, and on the walls the tablets to the memory of distinguished parishioners. Not a few of these old churches displayed in full view the royal arms in color, as may still be seen in the church of St. James, Goose Creek, near Charleston. Bells were on all the churches, for the colonists had come from England, "the most bellful country in the world," and they and their descendants preserved to the full their love for the sound of the bell, which summoned them to service, tolled for the dead, or marked at many hours the familiar routine of their daily life. Christ Church, Philadelphia, built in 1744, was distinguished by possessing a set of chimes.

Many a church had its separate vestry and sheds; and in large numbers of Southern parishes there were chapels of ease, small and built of wood, for those whose habitations were so remote that they could not come to the main church. Even so modest a structure as that at Pittsylvania Court House in Virginia — built of wood, with a clapboard roof, a plank floor, a pulpit and desk, two doors, five windows, a small table and benches —

had its chapel of ease built of round logs, with a clapboard roof and benches.

Though the New England minister was given a permanent call only after he had been tried as a candidate for half a year or some such period, the Anglican clergyman was generally appointed without regard to the wishes of the parishioners, often by the Society for the Propagation of the Gospel as one of its missionaries, in Maryland by the Proprietor, in the royal colonies by the Governor. Many of these clergymen were possessed of superior culture and godly piety and lived in harmony with their vestries and people; but in the South and in the West Indies to an extent greater than in New England, men of inferior ability and character crept into the rectorships and proved themselves incompetent as spiritual guides and unworthy as spiritual examples. But the proved instances of backsliding south of Maryland are not many and one ought not from isolated examples to infer the spiritual incompetency of the mass of the clergy in a colony. On the other hand it is not always safe to take the letters which the missionaries wrote home to the Venerable Society as entirely reliable evidence of their character and work, else the account would show no defects and the burden of defense would rest wholly with the colonists. John Urmston of Albemarle, for example, is known to North Carolinians as a "quarrelsome, haughty, and notoriously wicked clergyman," yet Governor Eden gave him a good character and the Society was satisfied that the fault lay with the country and the vestry. Clement Hall of St. Paul's Church, Edenton, was found to have officiated less than twenty-five Sundays in the year 1755; his salary was reduced accordingly and a new arrangement was made whereby he was to be paid only for what he did; yet Hall was looked upon as one of the most devoted and hard-working missionaries that the Society ever sent to America. Fithian speaks of Parson Gibbern of Virginia as "up three nights successively, drinking and playing at cards," and he characterizes Sunday there as "a day of pleasure and amusement," when "the gentlemen go to church as a matter of convenience and account the church a useful weekly resort to do business," yet this testimony, as the observation of a graduate of the College of New Jersey and a not unprejudiced witness, must be construed for what it is worth.

With the clergy in Maryland the case was somewhat different, and the illustrations of unspiritual

conduct are too numerous to be ignored.   Mayna-
dier of Talbot County was called "a good liver"
but a "horrid preacher," and his curate a "brute
of a parson."   William Tibbs of St. Paul's parish,
Baltimore County, was charged by his vestry with
being a common drunkard, and Henry Hall was on
one occasion "much disguised with liquor to the
great scandal" of his "function and evil examples
to others."   The people of St. Stephen's parish,
Cecil County, complained that their rector was
drunk on Sundays, and Bennet Allen, the notorious
rector of All Saints, Frederick County, who afterwards fought a duel with a brother of Daniel Dulaney in Hyde Park, London, was not only a cold-
blooded seeker of benefices but, according to many
of his parishioners, was guilty of immorality also.
The letters of Governor Sharpe disclose numerous
other cases of "scandalous behavior," "notorious
badness," "immoral conduct," and "abandoned
and prostituted life and character" on the part of
these unfaithful pastors; and by witness of even
the clergy themselves the establishment of Maryland deserved to be despised because "it permitted
clerical profligacy to murder the souls of men."
The situation reached its climax in the years
following 1734, when, by the withdrawal of the

Bishop of London's commissary, all discipline from the higher authorities of the Anglican Church was removed and the granting of livings was left solely in the hand of the dissolute Frederick Lord Baltimore until 1771, when, after the death of that degenerate proprietor, the Assembly was able to pass a law subjecting the clergy to rigid scrutiny and to the imposition of punishment in case of guilt.

On the whole it is probably safe to say that there was less religious seriousness and probity of conduct among the Southern clergy and parishioners than among the parsons and people of New England. One cannot easily imagine a New England woman writing as did Mrs. Burgwin of Cape Fear: "There is a clergyman arrived from England with a mission for this parish; he came by way of Charles Town and has been in Brunswick these three weeks. No compliment to his parishioners; but he is to exhibit here next Sunday. His size is said to be surprisingly long, I hope he is good in proportion."

Sermons occupied a less conspicuous place in the Anglican service than in those of other denominations. The lay reader did not preach, and the sermons of the ordained clergyman were not often more than fifteen or twenty minutes in length.

They seem to have been carefully prepared and many are spoken of in terms of high approval; they dwelt, however, less upon the infirmities of the flesh and more upon the abiding grace of God and the duties and functions of the Church. They were therefore rarely denunciatory or threatening but partook of the character of learned essays, frequently pedantic and overladen with classical allusions or quotations from the theological treatises written by the clergy in England. Not only were sermons provided for by will, as in the North, but they were also preached before the House of Burgesses in Virginia — which unlike most legislative bodies in the colonies had its chaplain — before Masonic lodges, and to the militia on Muster Day. Thomas Bray, commissary for Maryland, had many sermons printed, and the Reverend Thomas Bacon, to whom Maryland owes the earliest collection of her laws, printed four sermons preached in St. Peter's Church, Talbot County, two to "black slaves" and two for the benefit of a charitable school in the county. But the number of printed sermons in the South was not nearly as large as in the North.

It was not only in matters of ritual and vestments that the Anglican churches differed from those of nearly all the other denominations. While New England was engaging in a bitter controversy over the introduction of musical instruments into its public worship as well as what was styled the new way of singing by note instead of by rote, the leading Anglican churches were adding richness and beauty to their services by the use of organs and the employment of trained organists from England. The first organ used for religious purposes in the colonies was that bequeathed by Thomas Brattle, of Boston, to the Congregational Church of Brattle Square in 1713.[1] But, as that society "did not think it proper to use the same in the public worship of God," the organ, according to the terms of the will, went to King's Chapel, where it was thankfully received. This instrument, after a new organ had been purchased for King's Chapel in 1756, was transferred to Newburyport and finally to Portsmouth, where it is still preserved. In 1728 subscriptions were invited for a small organ to be placed in Christ Church, Philadelphia, but probably the purchase was never made, though it is known that both Christ Church

[1] The Reverend Joseph Green of Salem was in Boston on May 29, 1711, and while there heard an organ played. The instrument was undoubtedly that of Brattle. Essex Institute, *Historical Collections*, vol. x, p. 90.

and St. Peter's in that city had organs before the
Revolution. Bishop Berkeley gave an organ to
Trinity Church, Newport, as early as 1730, and six
years later an organist "who plays exceedingly fine
thereon" arrived and entered upon his work. The
organ loft in Christ Church, Cambridge, was a
very fine specimen of Georgian correctness and
grace, superior in its beauty to anything of its
kind in the colonies at that time. The first organ
in the South was installed in 1752 in Bruton Church,
Williamsburg, and Peter Pelham, Jr., whose father
married as his second wife the mother of Copley
the painter, was the first organist. All the organs
used in colonial times, however, were very small,
light in tone, and deficient in pipes.

CHAPTER VIII

THE PROBLEM OF LABOR

THE problem of obtaining labor in a frontier country where agriculture is the main pursuit was, in
colonial days as at the present, a difficult one, for
the employer could not go into a labor market and
hire what he pleased, since a labor market did not
exist. For this reason labor was always scarce in
America during this early period, and all sorts of
ways had to be contrived to meet the demand for
"help," particularly in the Middle and Northern
colonies. The farmers, who constituted the bulk
of the population, solved the problem in part by
doing their own work with the assistance of
their wives and children and such men as could be
hired for the busy seasons of planting and harvest-
ing. Such hired help was usually obtained in the
neighborhood and was paid in many ways — in
money, food, clothing, return labor, and orders on
the country store. It was never very steady nor

very reliable. On special occasions, such as raising the framework of a barn, house, school, or meetinghouse, all the neighbors turned out and helped,
satisfied with the rum, cider, and eatables furnished for refreshment. Necessary household service was supplied either by some woman of the
locality who came in as a favor and on terms of
equality with the rest of the family, or by a young
girl bound out as a servant, with the consent of her
father or mother, until she was of age.

Skilled labor was not often called for, except
in the towns or for shipbuilding, as the farmers
were their own shoemakers, coopers, carpenters,
tanners, and ironworkers, and even at times
their own surveyors, architects, lawyers, doctors,
and surgeons. Nearly every one was a jack at
many trades, for just as the minister physicked and
bled as well as preached, so the farmer could on
occasion run a store, build a house, make a boat,
and fashion his own farming utensils. [1] His house

[1] Joshua Hempstead of New London, for example, was not only a
farmer but at one time or another, from 1711 to 1758, a housebuilder,
carpenter, and cabinetmaker, shipwright, cobbler, maker of coffins,
and engraver of tombstones; a town official holding the offices of
selectman, treasurer, assessor, and surveyor of highways; a colony
official, serving as deputy sheriff and coroner, many times deputy to
the General Court, justice of the peace, and so performing frequent
marriages, and judge of probate. He was also clerk of the ecclesiastical

was a manufactory as well as a residence, and his barn a workshop as well as a place for hay and livestock. Of course as the eighteenth century wore on and men of the Huguenot type, with their love for beauty and good craftsmanship, came into the country, and as social life became more elaborate and luxurious, industrial activities were organized to meet the growing demands of a prosperous population. Artisans became more skilled and individual, and a few of them attained sufficient importance to occupy places of some dignity in the community and to produce works of such merit as to win repute in the history of arts and crafts in America. But these cases are exceptional; labor as a rule was not highly specialized, and the artisan usually added to his income in other ways. We find among the trades farriers, blacksmiths, whitesmiths, joiners, cabinetmakers, tailors, shipwrights, millwrights, gunsmiths, silversmiths, jewelers, watch and clock makers, and wig and peruke makers. For such highly skilled industries as snuff making, sugar refining, and glass blowing labor was imported

---

society, lieutenant and later captain of the train band, and surveyor of lands. He did a great deal of legal business, drawing deeds, leases, wills, and other similar documents, and was general handy man for his community.

from England, but not on any large scale until just before the Revolution, when agreements not to import English merchandise stimulated domestic manufacture.

Throughout the colonies the people as a whole depended not on hired labor but on bound labor — the indentured servant, the apprentice, the convict, and the slave — and everywhere these forms of labor appear in varying degrees.

The covenanted or indentured servant was one who engaged himself for a certain number of years in order to work off a debt. In itself such bond-service involved no special disgrace, any more than did going to prison for debt seriously discredit many of the fairly distinguished men who at one time or another were residents of the old Fleet Prison in London or those men of less repute who for the same reason found themselves in colonial jails. The reader must dismiss the notion that the position of an indentured servant necessarily involved degradation or that the term "sold" used in that connection referred to anything else than the selling of the time during which the individual was bound.[1] It was not uncommon for one

[1] The writer has seen a manuscript diary of a German servant who came to America by way of Rotterdam, in which the words

imprisoned for debt in the colonies to advertise his services to any one who would buy him out; and sometimes this form of service was used to pay a gambling debt.

But the most frequent form of indenture was that which bound the emigrant from England or the Continent to the captain of the ship on which he sailed. The captain paid the passage of the emigrant, furnished him with all necessary clothes, meat, drink, and lodging during the voyage, and then sold his time and labor on the ship's arrival in port. People went to the colonies in this way by the thousands and were to be found in every colony including the West Indies, although Georgia seems to have had on the whole very few. They were of all nationalities, but Germans, Swiss, English, Scotch, Irish, and Welsh predominated, with an occasional Frenchman. Probably the largest number were Germans, for the majority of those who came over were extremely poor and had to sell their time and that of their children to pay for their passage. Such methods continued for many years even after the Revolution.

"sell" and "sold," though used merely in the sense of binding to service, have been carefully erased by an outraged and uninformed descendant and the seemingly less invidious terms "hire" and "hired" inserted in their place.

German servants were shipped from Rotterdam, and British from Gravesend and other ports. To prevent enticing or kidnapping, all servants were registered before sailing and sometimes, as at Bristol, where the mayor and aldermen interfered, the ship was searched before sailing, the passengers were ordered ashore, and all who wished were released. When the vessel reached its American destination, word was spread or an advertisement was inserted in the newspapers saying that the indentures of a certain number of servants, men, women, and children, were available, and then the bargaining went on either aboard the ship or on shore at some convenient point to which the servants were taken. Such selling of indentures took place at all ports of entry from Boston to Charleston and gave rise to a brutal class of men popularly known as "soul drivers," who "made it their business to go on board all ships who have in either servants or convicts and buy sometimes the whole and sometimes a parcel of them as they can agree, and then they drive them through the country like a parcel of sheep, until they can sell them to advantage."[1]

The men thus disposed of for four to seven years ranged from sixteen to forty years of age

[1] Harrower's "Diary," *American Historical Review*, vol. vi, p. 77.

and brought from sixteen to twenty-four pounds. Children began the period of their service sometimes at the early age of ten. The abilities of these imported servants varied greatly: many were laborers, others were artisans and tradesmen, and a few were trained workmen possessed of exceptional skill. Among them were dyers, tailors, upholsterers, weavers, joiners, carpenters, cabinetmakers, barbers, shoemakers, peruke makers, whitesmiths, braziers, blacksmiths, coachmen, gentlemen's servants, gardeners, bakers, house waiters, schoolteachers, and even doctors and surgeons. Many could fence or could perform on some musical instrument, and one is described as professing "dancing, fencing, writing, arithmetic, drawing of pictures, and playing of legerdemain or slight of hand tricks." Benjamin Harrower, who served in America as clerk, bookkeeper, and schoolmaster, was an indentured servant, and so was Henry Callister, a Manxman, who was an assistant to the merchant Robert Morris, of Oxford, Maryland, and whose account books, preserved in the Maryland Diocesan Library, are today such a valuable source of information. Many of these servants were well-born but for offenses or for other reasons had to leave England: Jean Campbell, for instance, was related "to the very best families in Ayrshire"; William Gardner was the son of a Shropshire gentleman; John Keef claimed to have been an officer in the British Army; William Stevens and Thomas Lloyd of Virginia, who wrote home with regret of their former "follies," were evidently of good families; while the "light finger'd damsel" who ransacked the baggage of William Byrd, 2d, was a baronet's daughter sent to America as an incorrigible. Doubtless there were many such, though the total number could hardly have been large enough to affect the general statement that the indentured servant was of humble origin.

Many of these servants came over with the expectation that relatives or friends would redeem them, and in cases where these hopes were not realized the captain would advertise that unless some one appeared to pay the money the men or women would be sold. The indenture was looked upon as property which could even be bought by more than one purchaser, each of whom had a proportionate right to the servant's time, which could be sold, leased, and bequeathed by will, and which in the case of the sale or lease of a farm or plantation could be transferred to the buyer or tenant. Sometimes a colony, through the Governor, would buy the time of white servants for service in the militia or for work on the defenses of the province. It not infrequently happened that a master allowed a servant to exercise his trade at large through the colony, as in the case of Stephen Tinoe, a servant of one of the Virginia planters, who had dancing schools at Hampton, Yorktown, and Williamsburg, but who handed over to his master all the money which he received for his instruction. When the time named in the indenture expired, the servant became free, and the master was obliged to furnish him with a suit of clothes and to pay certain "freedom dues." There are many instances of servants bringing suit in the courts and contending that their masters were keeping them beyond their lawful time or had failed to give them their perquisites.

Inevitably under such a system the lot of the servants became very hard as the years passed and their status for the period of their service grew to be little better than that of slaves. While in the North they were usually treated with kindness and their position was not as irksome as it was in the South, yet in Maryland, Virginia, and the West Indies they suffered much abuse and degradation. William Randal of Maryland said in 1755 that the colony was a hard one for servants to live in, and

Elizabeth Sprigs wrote of "toiling day and night, and then tied up and whipped to that degree you would not beat an animal, scarce anything but Indian corn and salt to eat and that even begrudged." Governor Mathew of the Leeward Islands spoke of them as "poorly cladd, hard fedd, a worse state than a common soldier." As early as 1716 these indentured servants were called runaway thieves, disorderly persons, renegadoes, a loose sort of people, cheap and useless, and were said to grow more and more lazy, indolent, and impudent. Even in the North the later arrivals were deemed greatly inferior to those of the earlier years — a falling off which one observer ascribed to the want of good land wherewith to attract the better sort who desired to become farmers after serving their time.

There is no doubt that indentured servants in general made very poor laborers. The Irish Roman Catholics especially were feared and disliked and were not bought if others could be obtained. It is not to be wondered at that indentured servants were continually running away. The newspapers, North and South, were full of advertisements for the fugitives, describing their features, their clothes, and whatever they carried, for many of them made off with anything they could lay their hands on — horses, guns, household goods, clothing, and money. All sorts of laws were made, particularly in the South, to control these indentured servants. Should they absent them-selves from service without permission, they had to remain so many days longer in bondage; should they run away, they were liable to be whipped and to have their time extended; should a female serv-ant have a child, she was punished and the master of the child's father was required to pay for the time lost by the mother. In Virginia a freed serv-ant was obliged to have a ticket or certificate of freedom and if found without one was liable to arrest and imprisonment.

In addition to indentured servants there were also apprentices, usually children bound out to a master, until they were of age, by their poor parents to serve at some lawful employment or to learn a trade. There was nothing, however, to hinder a servant, or even a negro, from being bound out as an apprentice. Colonial apprenticeship, except in its educational features, was simply the system of England transferred to America, and the early indentures, of which there are copies extant for nearly all the colonies, were almost word for word the same as those of the mother country. Such apprenticeship was more than merely a form of labor; it was also a method of educating the poor and of implanting good morals. The apprentice on the one hand was bound to serve his master faithfully and to avoid taverns, alehouses, playhouses, unlawful games, and illicit amours; and the master on the other hand was obliged to provide his apprentice with food and lodging and to teach him to read and write and in the case of a doctor "to dismiss said apprentice with good skill in arithmetic, Latin and also in the Greek through the Greek Grammer."[1] A girl apprentice was to be taught "housewifery, knitting, spinning, sewing, and such like exercises as may be fitting and becoming her sex." At the end of the apprenticeship, the master was expected to give his apprentice two suits of clothes as a perquisite; but in the case of one girl he gave a cow, and of another "two suits of wearing apparel, one for Sunday and one for weekly labor, with two pairs of hose and shoes,

[1] Working one's passage to the medical profession was the only way in which a medical education could be obtained in America at this time. The first hospital, at Philadelphia, was not founded until 1751, and the first medical school, also at Philadelphia, not until 1765, and admission to that required a year's apprenticeship in a doctor's office.

two hoods or hats, or such headgear as may be comely and convenient, with all necessary linen." Sometimes an apprentice was scarcely to be distinguished from an indentured servant, as for instance when a minor bound himself to serve until a debt was paid off. Apprenticeship proved a useful sort of service in the colonies, for, though it was at times much abused and both masters and apprentices complained that the contracts were not carried out, it trained good workmen and satisfied a real need.

Though originally in quite a different position, the transported prisoner was in much the same condition as the servant and apprentice, for he too was a laborer bound to service without pay for a given number of years. Persons transported for religious or political reasons were few in number as compared with the convicts sent from Newgate and other British prisons and known as "transports," "seven year passengers," and "King's prisoners." Not less than forty thousand of these convicts were sent between the years 1717 and 1775 to the colonies, chiefly to Pennsylvania, Maryland, Virginia, and the West Indies. Some were transported for seven years, some for fourteen, and some for life, and though the colonies protested and those most nearly concerned passed laws against the practice, the need of labor was so great that convicts continued to be received and were sometimes even smuggled across the borders of the colony. Determined to get rid of an undesirable social element, England hoped in this way to lessen the number of executions at home and to turn to good account the skill and physical strength of able-bodied men and women. When a certain Englishman argued in favor of transporting felons for the purpose of reforming them, Franklin is said to have retaliated by suggesting the reformation of American rattlesnakes by sending them to England.

As convicts were often transported for very slight offenses, it is stated that, at times when conditions were very bad in the mother country, the starving poor, rather than continue to suffer, would commit trifling thefts for which transportation was the penalty. Thus though there were many who were confirmed criminals, those who had been merely petty offenders were distinctly advantageous to the colonies as artisans and laborers. Men and women alike were transported either in regular merchant ships or in vessels specially provided by contractors, who were paid by the Government from three to five pounds a head. Besides the ordinary passengers, indentured servants and convicts were frequently on the same ship and would be advertised for sale at the same time. Before the voyage was over, however, exciting things sometimes happened: one case is on record where the convicts mutinied, killed captain and ship's company, and sailed away on a piratical cruise; and another mutiny was foiled by shooting the ringleaders. On arrival at port the convict's time was sold exactly as was that of the indentured servant, and on the plantations both worked side by side with the negro. At the expiration of his term of service the convict was free to acquire land or to work as a hired laborer. As a rule, however, he preferred to return to England, where he frequently fell again into evil ways and was transported a second time to America.

The story is told of a barrister who had been caught stealing books from college libraries in Cambridge and had been sentenced to transportation without the privilege of returning to England. Though it was customary for the commoner sort of prisoners to be conducted on foot, with a sufficient guard, from Newgate to Blackfriars Stairs, whence they were carried in a closed lighter to the ship at Blackwall, this barrister and four other prisoners, including an attorney, a butcher, and a member of a noble family, were allowed to ride in hackney coaches with their keepers. Because the five were able to pay for their passage, they were treated on board ship with marks of respect and distinction. While the felons of inferior note were immediately put under hatches and confined in the hold of the ship, the five privileged malefactors were conveyed to the cabin which they were to have for the duration of the voyage. "It is supposed," says the narrator, "that as soon as they land they will be set at liberty, instead of being sold as felons usually are, and that thus a criminal who has money may blunt the edge of justice and make that his happiness which the law designs as his punishment."

Though many convicts became useful laborers and farmers, others were a continual nuisance and even danger to the colonists. They ran away, committed robberies, — "poor unhappy wretches who cannot leave off their old trade," they are called — turned highwaymen, set houses on fire, engaged in counterfeiting, and were guilty even of murder. In the West Indies they corrupted the negroes and lured them off on piratical expeditions. Governor Hunter wrote from Jamaica in 1731 that people who had been accustomed to sleep with their doors open were obliged, since the arrival of the convicts, "to keep watches on their counting and store houses," since several robberies had recently been committed. Many were caught and imprisoned; others, when convicted a second time, were hanged. The convicts were an ill-featured crew, often pock-marked, sly and cunning, and garbed in all sorts of nondescript clothing, and whether at home or at large their evil propensities and uncleanly habits, together with their proneness to contagious diseases and jail fever, made them a menace to masters and communities alike.

Negroes, the mainstay of labor on the plantations of the South and the West Indies, differed from indentured servants in that their bodies as well as their time and labor were bartered and sold. Though the servant's loss of liberty was temporary, that of the negro was perpetual. Yet in the seventeenth century negroes were viewed in the light of servants rather than of slaves, and it is noteworthy how rarely the word "slave" was used in common parlance at that early period. But by the eighteenth century perpetual servitude had become the rule. Indeed, so essential did it become that before long few indentured servants were to be found on the tobacco plantations and rice fields of the South, for their places had been everywhere taken by the negroes. Though in Maryland, Virginia, and North Carolina the whites outnumbered the blacks two or three times to one, in South Carolina and the West Indies the reverse was the case, for there the blacks outnumbered the whites ten and twenty fold.

The negroes came from the western coast of Africa, north as far as Senegambia and south as far as Angola, where lay the factories and "castles" of those engaged in the trade. For Great Britain the business of buying negroes was in the hands of the Royal African Company until 1698, when the monopoly was broken and the trade was thrown open to private firms and individual dealers who controlled the bulk of the business in the eighteenth century. The independent traders were both British and colonial — the former from London, Bristol, and Liverpool, the latter from Boston, Newport, New York, Charleston, and other seaports — who brought their negroes direct from Africa or bought them in the West Indies for sale in the colonies. The voyage of a slaver was a dangerous and gruesome experience, and the "Guinea captains," as they were called, were often truculent, inhuman characters.

The negroes were obtained either at the African Company's factories or from the native chiefs and African slave drivers in exchange for all sorts of cloths, stuffs, hardware, ammunition, and for rum of inferior quality made especially for this trade. The slaves were taken to America chained between decks during the passage, a treatment so brutal that many died or committed suicide on the voyage. In such close and unhealthy confinement epidemics were frequent, and diseases were so often communicated to the white sailors that the mortality on board was usually high — ordinarily from five to ten per cent and sometimes running to more than thirty under particularly unfavorable circumstances. Many cases are recorded of uprisings in which whole crews were murdered and captains and mates tortured and mutilated in revenge for their cruelty.

Male negroes from fifteen to twenty years of age were most in demand, because women were physically less capable and the older negroes were more inclined to moroseness and suicide. Those from the Gold Coast, Windward Coast, and Angola were as a rule preferred, because they were healthier, bigger, and more tractable; those from Gambia were generally rated inferior, though opinions differed on this point; and those from Calabar, if over seventeen, were not desired because they were given to melancholy and self-destruction. All were brought over naked, but they often received clothing before their arrival, partly for decency's sake and partly for protection against the cold and the water coming through the decks. Some prejudice existed against negroes from the West Indies who spoke English, because they were believed to be great rogues and less amenable to discipline than were the American-born, who always brought higher prices because they could stand the climate and were used to plantation work.

In the North, at Boston and Newport, the negroes were sold directly to the purchaser by the captain or owner, or else were disposed of through the medium of advertisements and intelligence offices. But in Virginia and South Carolina they were more frequently sold in batches to the local merchants, by whom they were bartered singly or in groups of two or three, to the planters for tobacco, rice, indigo, or cash. They were frequently taken to fairs, which were a favorite place for selling slaves. Probably the most active market in the colonies, however, was at Charleston, where many firms were engaged in the Guinea business, either on their own account or as agents for British houses. Henry Laurens, a "negro merchant" from 1748 to 1762, has given in his letters an admirable account of the way in which negroes were handled in that city. Planters sometimes came seventy miles to purchase slaves and "were so mad after them that some of them went to loggerheads and bid so upon each other that some very fine men sold for £300" in colonial currency, or £40 sterling. "Some of the buyers went to collaring each other and would have come to blows," and, adds Laurens, by the number of purchasers he saw in town he judged that a thousand slaves would not have supplied their wants. Every effort was made to prevent the spread of disease, and vessels with plagues on board were often quarantined or the negroes removed to pens to guard against contagion. In spite of this, however, many negroes arrived "disordered" or "meager," with sore eyes and other ailments. Those that were healthy and not too small were kept in pens or yards until brought to the auction block. The amount for which they were sold depended on the state of the crops and the price of rice and indigo.

As soon as the negroes were purchased, they were taken to the plantation and put to work in the

tobacco, rice, and indigo fields or were employed
about the house at tasks of a more domestic character. In the North they served as household servants or on the farm, clearing the woods and cul-
tivating lands. Some were coachmen, boatmen,
sailors, and porters in shops and warehouses.
As many of them became in time skillful shoemakers, coopers, masons, and blacksmiths, they
not only did the heavier work incident to these
crafts but at the same time became something of
a financial asset to their owners, who hired them
out to other planters, contractors, and even the
Government, and then pocketed the wages themselves. In Newport hired slaves aided in building
the Jewish synagogue; in Williamsburg the slaves
of Thomas Jones made shoes for people of the
town; and in Charleston large numbers of slaves
were employed to work on the fortifications. They
had their own quarters to live in, both on the plantations and in certain sections of the towns, and
even the domestic servants, commonly in the South
and occasionally in the North, had shanties of their
own. The clothing which the slaves wore was
always coarse in texture; their bedding was scanty,
merely coarse covers or cheap blankets bought
specially for the purpose; and their food consisted

of corn bread, ash cake, rice, beans, bacon, beef on rare occasions, butter, and milk.

The slaves in domestic service were well cared for, and Laurens once said that his negroes were "as happy as slavery will admit of; none run away and the greatest punishment to a defaulter is to sell him." Van Cortlandt of New York offered for sale a valuable negro woman who had been in his family a number of years and could do all kinds of work. "I would not take two hundred pounds for her," he wrote, "if it were not for her impudence; but she is so intorabel saucy to her mistress." Thomas Jones once wrote to his wife: "Our family is in as much disorder with our servants as when you left it and worse, Venus being so incorigable in her bad habits and her natural ill disposition that there will be no keeping her"; and later he added: "There is no dependence on negroes without somebody continually to follow them." Dr. McSparran records in his diary how he was obliged to whip his negroes and how even his wife, "my poor passionate dear," gave them a lash or two. On the other hand in many instances the devotion of negro servants to their masters, mistresses, and the children of the family is well attested, and many were freed for their continued good service and faithful loyalty.

They had their pleasures, were fond of dancing and music, attained considerable skill as dancing masters and players on the fiddle and French horn, and in South Carolina were even allowed to carry guns and hunt provided their masters obtained tickets or licenses for them.

The field hands suffered from their condition more than did those who served on the place or in the house. The work which they had to do was heavier and more exhausting, and the treatment which they received was far less kindly and considerate. For the cruelty to negroes the overseers were largely responsible, though the planters themselves were not exempt from blame. In the case of a master murdered by his slaves, the opinion was widely expressed that, as he had shown no mercy to them, he could expect none himself. Whipping to death was a not uncommon punishment, and in one case an overseer and his assistant in Virginia were hanged for this offense as murder. A South Carolinian who killed a negro "in a sudden heat of passion" was fined fifty pounds, and Quincy reports that in the same colony, though to steal a negro was punishable by death, to kill him was only finable, no matter how wanton the act might be. Many illustrations could be given of cruel treatment — such as suspension over a sharpened peg in the floor as a means of extracting a secret, or scraping the back with a currycomb and rubbing salt into the wounds, a procedure known as "pickling" — but the list is too long and harrowing. It is recorded that a negro who took part in the New York uprising of 1712 was hanged alive in chains. A negro who committed arson or who killed another negro was ordinarily hanged and quartered. One who murdered his master or mistress was burned at the stake, for such murder was construed as petty treason. In Massachusetts, New York, New Jersey, Virginia, North and South Carolina, and the West Indies negroes were burned alive for various crimes. In one South Carolina case, the negro who was burned had set fire to the town on a windy night. Negroes were castrated for rape; one for attempted assault on a white child was whipped around the town at a cart's tail; and another for a lesser crime was sentenced to be "whipped and pickled around Charles Town square."

Negroes were almost as frequent runaways as were the convicts and indentured servants. If they resisted when caught, they (in South Carolina at least) might be shot about the breech with

small or swan shot. They were put in jail with
felons and debtors or in the workhouse, where they
were "corrected" at fifteen shillings a week and
returned to their masters. They frequently fled
to the back country or attempted to escape to sea
by passing themselves off to the captains of ships
as free negroes.

Miscegenation was probably very common. Instances of white women giving birth to black children, and of white men living with colored women
are rare but nevertheless are occasionally met with.
Joseph Pendarvis of Charleston left his property
to his children by a negro woman, Parthenia, "who
had lived with him for many years," and the will
may be seen today among the records of the probate court of Charleston. Indeed so scandalous
did such illicit intercourse become in South Carolina, that the grand jury of 1743 presented the
"too common practice of criminal conversation
with negro and other slave wenches as an enormity
and evil of general ill-consequence," and Quincy
bears witness to the prevalence of this practice
when he says that it was "far from uncommon to
see a gentleman at dinner and his reputed offspring
a slave to the master of the table."

CHAPTER IX

COLONIAL TRAVEL

THE vast body of colonists stayed at home. They lived quiet and uneventful lives, little disturbed by the lust for travel and seldom interrupted by journeys from their place of abode. There were, of course, always those whose business took them from one colony to another or over the sea to the West Indies or to England; there were the thousands, north and south, who at one time or another went from place to place in an effort to improve their condition; and, finally, there were the New Englanders, the Germans, and the Scotch-Irish who, in ever-increasing numbers, wandered westward towards the uplands and the frontier, led on by that unconquerable restlessness which always seizes upon settlers in a new land.

Of these the most enterprising wanderers and the forerunners of the tourists of today were the voyagers overseas to England, the Continent, and the West Indies for business, education, health, and pleasure. Many who went to England on colonial employment or for education, took advantage of the opportunity to see the sights or to make the "grand tour" of the Continent. One of the earliest of New Englanders to visit the Continent was John Checkley of Boston, who studied at Oxford and traveled in Europe before 1710. Another was Thomas Bulfinch, whose father wrote to him in Paris in 1720: "I am glad of your going there, it being, I doubt not for your good, though somewhat chargeable." Elizabeth, wife of Colonel Thomas Jones, who went abroad in 1728 for her health, had one of her husband's London correspondents look after her, provide her with money, arrange for her baggage, and purchase what was needful. She stayed for a time in London, where she consulted Sir Hans Sloane, went to Bath, where she took the waters, and was gone from home nearly two years. Laurens went to England in 1749, a nine weeks' voyage, to study the conditions of trade, and traveled on horseback to Manchester, Birmingham, Worcester, and other towns, where he was entertained by merchants to whom he had letters or with whom he did business. The many Virginians — Randolphs, Carters, and others

— who were at Gray's Inn or the Middle Temple, probably traveled elsewhere to some extent, while of the South Carolinians who visited Europe Ralph Izard went to Dijon, Geneva, Florence, Rome, Naples, and Strasbourg. Charles Carroll of Maryland was away from home at his studies and on his travels for sixteen years, living at St. Omer in France, studying law in England, visiting the Low Countries, and even planning to go to Berlin, which he did not reach, however, partly for lack of time and partly because he heard that the accommodations were bad and the roads were infested with banditti. Many members of the Baltimore family traveled widely; Copley the painter in 1774 went to Rome, Marseilles, Paris, and London; Boucher speaks of a "gentleman-clergyman" in Virginia who had made the grand tour and was exceedingly instructive and entertaining in his conversation; and doubtless there were many others who made trips to foreign cities but whose travels remain unrecorded. On the other hand members of English and Scottish families were often widely scattered throughout the colonial world and travelers from the British Isles would occasionally go from place to place in America visiting their relatives, trying new business openings, or seeking recovery of their health.

Those who visited only the British Isles were very numerous. The voyage from the colonies was not ordinarily difficult, though the dangers of the North Atlantic and inconveniences on shipboard in those days were sometimes very serious. "We had everything washed off our decks," wrote one who had just arrived in England, "and was once going to stove all our water and throw our guns and part of our cargo overboard to lighten the ship; four days and nights at one time under a reef mainsail, our decks never dry from the time we left Cape Henry." But despite the difficulties ships were constantly coming and going, and ample provision for passengers was made. The trip from London to Boston sometimes lasted only twenty-six days, and five weeks to the Capes was considered a fine passage. Chalkley, the Quaker, was eight weeks sailing from Land's End to Virginia, and Peckover nine weeks and five days from London to New York. An Irish traveler was forty-two days from Limerick to the same city. Sailing by the southerly route and into the Trades made a longer voyage but a pleasanter one, and those who were able to pay well for their cabins and to take extra provisions were in comfort compared with the servants and other emigrants, whose experiences below decks aft in the steerage during stormy and protracted voyages must have been harrowing in the extreme.

There was scarcely a merchant ship but took on passengers going one way or the other, and of the life on board we have many accounts.

Hundreds of colonists went to the West Indies to search for employment, to investigate commercial opportunities, to visit their plantations — for there were many who owned plantations in the islands — or merely to enjoy the pleasures of the trip. The voyage, which was in any case a comparatively short one, varied slightly according to the port of departure and the route. It usually occupied two weeks from the Northern colonies. David Mendes thought a trip of twenty-nine days from Newport to Jamaica a very dismal and melancholy passage, but another Rhode Islander in 1752 estimated a trip to the Bahamas and back, including the time necessary for selling and purchasing cargoes, at from two to three and a half months. In Virginia it was customary to sail from Norfolk, the center of that colony's trade with the West Indies.

Travel from one continental colony to another merely for pleasure was not of frequent occurrence,

ONE-HORSE CHAISE OF ABOUT 1780

In the Essex Institute, Salem, Mass. This is said to be the only chaise of the Revolutionary period in any museum.

ONE-HORSE CHAISE OF ABOUT 1780

In the Essex Institute, Salem, Mass. This is said to be the only chaise
of the Revolutionary period in any museum

as far as the colonists themselves were concerned. It was more common for men and women from the South and the West Indies to visit the North to recover their health and to enjoy the cooler climate than it was for the Northerners to go southward. William Byrd, 3d, and his wife planned to travel in the North in 1763, and in 1770 thirty-two people from South Carolina went to Philadelphia, New York, Newport, and Boston either as invalids or as tourists. Men on business were constantly moving about from colony to colony. Visitors from England, Scotland, and the West Indies made long journeys and were often lavishly entertained as they passed from town to town with letters of introduction from one official or merchant to another. James Birket of Antigua traveled from Portsmouth to the Chesapeake in 1750, and the record of his journey is a document of rare value in social history. Lowbridge Knight of Bristol went from Georgia to Quebec in 1764. The travels of George Whitefield, the preacher, Peter Kalm, the Swedish professor, Thompson, the S. P. G. missionary, and Burnaby, the Anglican clergyman, are well known.[1]

---

[1] Other interesting accounts will be found in the records of the Quakers Edmundson, Richardson, Chalkley, Fothergill, Wilson, Dickinson, Peckover, and Esther Palmer.

In 1764–1765, Lord Adam Gordon spent fifteen
months going from Antigua through the colonies
to Montreal and Quebec, returning by way of New
England to New York, whence he sailed for England.   In 1770 Sir William Draper made the tour,
with a party consisting of his nephew, his nephew's
wife, and a Mrs. Beresford.   The visit of these two
titled Britishers made a considerable stir in American society and was duly chronicled in the papers.
The impression made by Lord Adam and others
may be inferred from Mrs. Burgwin's remarks to
her sister: "In my last I was going to tell you
about the great people we had in town [Wilming-
ton], really a colection of as ugly ungenteal men
as I've seen, four in number.   Lord Adam is
tall, slender, of the specter kind intirely; Capt.
McDonnel a highlander very sprightly; the other
two are Americans just come from England where
they have been educated, both very rich, which will
no doubt make amends for every defect in Mr.
Izard and Wormly."

Travelers in the early part of the century were
obliged to go chiefly by water, and they continued
to use this method in the colonies south of Pennsylvania in which the wide rivers, bays, and
swamps rendered the land routes difficult and

dangerous. At all times, indeed, the waterways were quicker and less fatiguing, particularly in the case of long journeys. The travelers used the larger vessels, ships, pinks, barks, brigs, brigantines, snows, and bilanders, for ocean voyages and frequently for coastwise transportation from colony to colony.

For coastwise and West India trade the commoner colonial craft in use were shallops, sloops, and schooners, of which those built in New England were the best known. Bermuda sloops or sloops built after the Bermuda model, which were prime sailers and often engaged in the colonial carrying trade, were common in the South. For passage up and down inland waters such as the Hudson River and Chesapeake Bay, and for supplying the big merchant ships in Southern waters, sloops were the rule. Rafts contrived for carrying lumber and partly loaded before launching with timber so framed as to be almost solid, were floated down the rivers. For ordinary purposes — for transporting wood, lumber, tobacco, rice, indigo, and naval stores on shallow inland watercourses — the colonists used various kinds of flatboats, each with its boss or patroon and often carrying mainsail and jib for sailing before the wind. For short distances they used dingies, yawls, and longboats as well as canoes fashioned in many sizes and shapes — either dugouts or light craft made of cedar and cypress, propelled by paddles or oars, and in some cases fitted with thwarts and steps for masts and some even with cabins and forecastles.

Flat-bottomed "fall-boats" were used for freighting and passenger travel on the Connecticut River above Hartford, but they had no sleeping accommodations and passengers had to put up for the night at taverns along the route. Such wealthy planters as the Carters on the Rappahannock had family boats with four and six oars and awnings. The customs officials at all the large ports had rowboats and barges. Some of these craft were handsomely painted, and at New York, for example, carried sails, awnings, a coxswain, and bargemen in livery.

As the colonists made little provision for the improvement of navigation, shipwrecks were of all too frequent occurrence. Vessels ran ashore, grounded on sand bars, or went to pieces on shoals and reefs. Many lighthouses were built between 1716 and 1775, chiefly of brick and from fifty to one hundred and twenty feet high, but the lights were poor and unreliable. The earliest beacon showed oil lamps in a lantern formed of close-set window sashes. The most important early lights were in Boston Harbor, off Newport, on Sandy Hook, on Cape Henry, in Middle Bay Island, Charleston, and on Tybee Island, Savannah, and toward the end of the period in Portsmouth Harbor and at Halifax. The Boston light had a glazed cage, roofed with copper and supported on a brick arch. The lamps had to be supplied with oil two or three times in the night and even though they were snuffed every hour the glass was never free from smoke. Not until the lighthouse at Halifax was erected in 1772 was a better system adopted. In many of the more important and dangerous channels, as at the eastern end of Long Island Sound, in the North Carolina inlets, and among the bars of the Southern rivers, buoys were placed, often at private expense, and everywhere pilots were required for the larger vessels entering New London, New York, and other harbors, passing through the Capes of Virginia, navigating Roanoke and Ocracock inlets, going up from Tybee to Savannah, and sometimes on the more dangerous reaches of the rivers.

As population increased and settlement was extended farther and farther westward from the region of coastwise navigation to areas not easily reached even from the rivers, the colonists were forced to depend more and more upon travel by land. Trails were widened into tote roads and bridle paths, and these in turn into carriage roads, until they grew into highways connecting towns with towns and colonies with colonies. The process of developing this vast system of pathways through the back country was slow, expensive, and very imperfect. Nothing but sheer necessity could have compelled men to drive these roads through the dense forests and tangled undergrowth, across marshes, and over rocky hills; nothing else could have made them endure the arduous and dangerous riding through "the howling wilderness," as the colonists themselves called it, particularly in the South and the back country, where the roads ran always through lonely woods. The menace of treacherous ground, falling trees, high river banks, and dangerous fords were real to every traveler. All the records of these early journeys refer to the ever present danger from the accidents and injuries of highway travel. In the South guides were particularly necessary, for to miss one's way was a harrowing and dangerous experience.

But necessity won the day. Tremendous advances were made in the eighteenth century, when the need of more rapid and extended communication by land became imperative and the postal service in particular was demanding better facilities. The colonies now made strenuous efforts to improve their roads, increase the number of their ferries, and build causeways and bridges wherever possible. New England soon became a network of roads and highways, with main routes connecting the important towns, country roads radiating from junction points, and lanes, pent roads, and private ways leading to outlying sections. Philadelphia became the terminus of such roads from the country behind it, as those running from Lancaster, York, Reading, and the Susquehanna. From Baltimore, Alexandria, Falmouth, and Richmond roads ran westward and joined the great wagon and cattle thoroughfare which stretched across Maryland and Virginia, by way of York, the Monocacy, Winchester, and Staunton, to the Indian country of the Catawbas, Cherokees, and Chickasaws.

The great intercolonial highways, which were also used as post roads, ran from Portsmouth to Savannah. Starting from Portsmouth in 1760, the traveler would first make his way over an excellent piece of smooth, hard-graveled road available for stage, carriage, or horse, southward to the Merrimac, which he would cross on a sailing ferry, and thence proceed by way of Ipswich to Boston. William Barrell started on this trip by stage in August, 1766, but, finding the vehicle too crowded for warm weather got out at Ipswich and finished the journey in a chaise. From Boston one would have the choice of four ways of going to New Haven: one by way of Providence to New London; a second by way of Providence, Bristol, and Newport, a troublesome journey involving three ferry crossings; a third over the Old Bay road to Springfield and thence south through Hartford and Meriden; and a fourth, much used by Connecticut people, diagonally through the northeastern part of the colony, crossing the dangerous Quinebaug and Shetuckit rivers, and reaching New Haven by way of either Hartford or Middletown. At Springfield, if the traveler wished, he could continue westward to Kinderhook and Albany along a road used by traders and the militia, or at Hartford he could take through northwestern Connecticut one of the newest and worst roads in New England, to be known later as the Albany turnpike. Lord Adam Gordon, who passed over this road in going from Albany to Hartford in 1765, described that section which ran through the

Greenwoods from Norfolk to Simsbury as "the worst road I have seen in America," and the colony itself so far agreed in 1758 as to consider it "ill-chosen and unfit for use and not sufficiently direct and convenient." Though efforts were made to repair it, the road remained for years very crooked and encumbered with fallen trees.

Once he had reached New Haven, the traveler would find that the road to New York, which stretched along the Sound, still required about two days of hard riding or driving. These Connecticut roads had indeed a bad reputation. The traveler's progress was interrupted by troublesome and even dangerous ferries and he frequently had to ride over much soft, rocky, and treacherous ground. Mrs. Knight described their terrors in 1704; Peckover says in 1743 that he "had abundance of very rough, stony, uneven roads"; Birket in 1750 calls parts of them "most intollerable" and "most miserable"; and Barrell on "old Sorrell" was nearly worn out by them sixteen years later. Though Cuyler of New York, who went over them to Rhode Island in 1757 in a curricle or two-horse chair, failed to complain of his journey, his good nature may be due to the fact that he went for a wife, "a very agreeable young lady with a gentle fortune." Quincy preferred to take boat from New York to Boston rather than face the inconveniences of these notorious roads. Many travelers took a sloop from Newport or New London, and by going to Sterling or Oyster Bay, in order to avoid the pine barrens in the center of Long Island, and proceeding thence to New York, they not only saved fifty miles but also had a better road. There was a ferry from Norwalk to Huntington, but that was chiefly for those who desired to go to Long Island without taking the roundabout journey through New York.

The traveler might go to Albany from New York, either by sloop or by road, preferably along the eastern bank. If he were going southward, he might select one of three ways. He could cross to Paulus Hook (now Jersey City) by ferry or could go to Perth Amboy by sloop through the Kill van Kull and Staten Island Sound, or by ferrying to Staten Island he could traverse the northern end of the island and take a second ferry to Elizabethport. Once on New Jersey soil, he would find two customary routes to Philadelphia: one by road to New Brunswick and Bordentown and down the Delaware by water; the other by the same road to Bordentown, thence by land to Burlington, and across the river by boat. In 1770 a stage company offered to make the trip in two days, and thus rendered it possible for a New York merchant to spend two nights and a day in Philadelphia on business and be back in five days, a rapid trip for the period.

Unless one were going into the back country by way of Lancaster and York southwestward or from Lancaster or Reading northwest to Fort Augusta (now Sunbury) and the West Branch, there was but one road which he could take in leaving Philadelphia. It ran by way of Chester along the Delaware, crossed the Brandywine toll-bridge to Wilmington, and ran on to Christiana bridge, the starting point for Maryland and the Chesapeake as well as the delivery center for goods shipped from Philadelphia for transfer to the Eastern and Western shores. Here the road divided: one branch went down the Eastern Shore to Chestertown, from which point the traveler might cross the Bay to Annapolis; the other rounded the head of the Bay, crossed the Susquehanna near Port Deposit, and so ran on to Joppa, Baltimore, and Annapolis. Birket tells of passing over the Susquehanna in January on the ice, and describes how the horses were led across and the party followed on foot, with the exception of two women who sat on ladders "and were drawn over by two men, who slipt off their shoes and run so fast that we could not keep way with them." From Annapolis the traveler could go directly to Alexandria by way of Upper Marlboro, or he could take a somewhat more southerly route to Piscataway Creek and thence across the Potomac by ferry until he reached the road from Alexandria to Richmond and proceeded southward by way of Dumfries and Fredericksburg. From Fredericksburg and Falmouth a road ran to Winchester through Ashby's Gap and was much used for hauling supplies northwest from the stores there and for bringing down flour and iron from the farms and Zane's iron works in the Shenandoah. From Richmond one might go directly to Williamsburg, cross the James at Jamestown by the Hog Island Ferry, and continue by a rough road through Nansemond County, skirting west of the Dismal Swamp to Edenton; or he might cross the James farther down the peninsula at Newport or Hampton, go to Norfolk by sloop, and thence continue south on the other side of the swamp by way of North River, and southwest through the Albemarle counties to the same destination. Another road which ran through Petersburg and Suffolk was sometimes used.

The traveling and postal routes south of Annapolis were much less fixed than those in the North, for transit by water was as frequent as by land, and the possible combinations of land and water routes were many and varied. According to the regulations of 1738, which for the first time established a settled mail service from the North to Williamsburg and Edenton, the postrider met the Philadelphia courier at the Susquehanna, rode thence to Annapolis, crossed the Potomac to New Post — the plantation of Governor Spotswood, the deputy postmaster-general, on the Rappahannock just below Fredericksburg — and ended his trip at Williamsburg, whence a stage carried the mail to Edenton by way of Hog Island Ferry and Nansemond Court House. The uncertainties of the Eastern Shore postal connections as late as 1761 can be judged from a letter which John Schaw wrote in that year: "You'll observe," he says, "how difficult it is to get a letter from you, that post office at Annapolis being a grave of all letters to this side of the Bay. I am sending this by way of Kent Island, and am in hopes it will get sooner to you than yours did to me."

From Edenton there was but a single road which ran as directly as possible to Charleston, but nevertheless it was long, arduous, and slow. There were many rivers to be crossed, including a five-mile ferry across Albemarle Sound, detours to be made around the wide mouths of the Pamlico and the Neuse, and much low and wet ground to be avoided. Frederick Jones took six days to go from Williamsburg to New Bern. Schoepf records how he was delayed at Edenton four days because the ferryman had allowed his negroes to go off with the boat on a pleasure excursion of their own — an indulgence which shows that even after the Revolution travelers in that section were few and far between. From New Bern to the Cape Fear or Wilmington was not a difficult journey, for Peter du Bois accomplished it on horseback in 1757 with no other comment than an expression of satisfaction at the fried chicken and eggs that he had for breakfast and the duck and fried hominy that he ate for dinner. From Wilmington, after ferrying over to Negro Head Point with bad boats and very poor service in 1764, the traveler might continue, by a lonely, desolate, and little frequented way, to Georgetown and Charleston. It was a noteworthy event in the history of the colonies when the first post stage was established in 1739 south of Edenton and postal communication was at last opened all the way from Portsmouth and Boston through the principal towns and places in New York, Pennsylvania, Maryland, Virginia, and North Carolina to Charleston, and even thence by the occasional services of private individuals to Georgia and points beyond. At Charleston, which was the distributing center for the far South, the road branched, and one line went back through Dorchester, Orangeburg Court House, and Ninety-Six, to the towns of the lower Cherokee, a route used by caravans and Indian traders; another turned off at Dorchester for Fort Moore and Fort Augusta on the upper Savannah; and a third curved away from the coast to Savannah to avoid the rivers and sounds of Beaufort County. In 1767 the mail was carried from Savannah to Augusta and on to Pensacola by way of St. Marks and Appalachicola, but the journeys were dangerous and sometimes the postman could not get through on account of raids by the Creek Indians.

Land travel before 1770 had become very common even in the South. Laurens wrote to John Rutherfurd of Cape Fear: "I believe you are the greatest traveler in America. You talk of a 400

mile ride as any other man would one of 40. I
hope these frequent long journeys will not prejudice your health." Laurens himself usually went
by boat to visit his plantations in Georgia — a
single day's journey instead of two by horseback;
but in 1769 he went off for seven weeks almost a
thousand miles through the woods to visit his up-
river properties. Governor Montagu in 1768 went
all the way from Boston to Charleston by land;
and the Anglican missionaries traveled long distances in Maryland, Virginia, and North Carolina
to visit their parishioners and baptize the children.
Merchants are known to have journeyed far to
collect their debts. Allason speaks of going from
forty to ninety miles from house to house on collecting tours; merchants who sold their goods "in
the lumping way" rode up and down the river
towns and plantations in their efforts to dispose of
their consignments; and itinerant pedlars, with
their horses and packs, wandered on from place to
place, South as well as North, retailing their wares.

Though journeying by land was at all times
an arduous experience, it was particularly difficult
during heavy rains and freshets, in the winter season, and when forest fires were burning. The
winters were as variable then as now. Often there

was no ice before February and many a green Christmas is recorded.[1] In other years the season would be one of prolonged cold, the winter of 1771–1772 having nineteen "plentiful effusions of snow." Checkley records a frost in Boston on June 14, 1735, and a snowstorm on the 30th of October in the same year. In December, 1752, the temperature in Charleston dropped from 70° to 24° in a single day, and there were many winters in the South when frost injured the crops and killed the orange blossoms. Once, in the winter of 1738, no mail reached Williamsburg for six weeks on account of the bad weather. Mrs. Manigault of Charleston notes in her diary that the burial of her daughter in February had to be postponed on account of the deep snow.

Rivers were crossed at fords whenever possible, but ferries were introduced from the first on the main lines of travel. All sorts of craft were utilized for crossing: canoes for passengers, flatboats and scows for horses and carriages, and sailing vessels,

[1] New England. "Feb. 12, 1703. Summer weather, no winter yet." Green's *Diary*. Yet on the 28th of September following there were two inches of snow. Preston in his diary says of the winter of 1754–1755: "This winter was open, no sledding at all." Essex Institute, *Historical Collections*, vol. VIII, p. 222; vol. XI, p. 258, note.

15

chiefly sloops, where the crossings were longer and therefore more dangerous. Rope ferries were necessary wherever the current was swift, though they were always an annoying obstruction on navigable rivers. At much traveled places two boats were frequently required, one on each bank. The ferryman was summoned usually by hallooing, by ringing a bell, or by building a fire in the marshes. Licenses for ferries were issued and rates were fixed by the Assembly in the North and the county court in the South. Passage was ordinarily free to the postrider and to public officials, and in Connecticut to children going to school, worshipers going to church, and sometimes to militia men on their way to musters.

Bridges over small streams were built before the end of the seventeenth century, but those over the larger rivers were late in construction, because as a rule the difficulties involved were too great for the colonial builders to cope with. Many of these bridges were the result of private enterprise, and toll was taken by permission of Assembly or court. First they were always built of timbers, in the form of "geometry work," with causeways. The raising of a bridge in New England was a public event, at which the people of the surrounding country

appeared to offer their services. Bridges constructed over such swift rivers as the Quinebaug
in Connecticut had to be renewed many times, as
they were frequently carried away by ice or freshets.
Stone bridges could be built only where the distances were short and the water was comparatively
shallow. Peter Kalm mentions two stone bridges
on the way from Trenton to Philadelphia.[1] There
was a very good wooden bridge over the Charles
River between Boston and Cambridge, and others
were built over the Mystic, the Quinnipiac, the
Harlem, the Brandywine, Christiana Creek, and

[1] One of these is described by another traveler as follows: "Sd
Bridge stands on two pillars of stone and arched over makes three
arches. The middlemost is something largest and is about 20 foot
wide. The river was low it having been a very dry time. I rid through
under the bridge up streem to view the under side. I counted the
stones that go round the mouth of one arch and there is sixty. One
arch hath eighty stones round the mouth of it. They seem all of a
size and seem to be about 18 inches long and 2 broad and six inches
thick. The lower end of each stone is much less than the upper end
and laid in lyme (as all the bridge is) and it looks in the shape of an
ovens mouth. The bridge is about 20 rod in length and gradually
rounding, the stones covered over on the top with earth and wide
enough for 2 or 3 carts to pass a breast. On each side is a stone wall
built up about 3 foot and an half, a flat hewn stone on the top about
4 foot in length and 12 or 14 inches wide and about 4 inches thick and
an iron staple let in to each joynt, one part of said staple in one stone
and the other part of said staple in the other stone, and 80 stones
covers the wall on one side which I counted and the other I suppose
the same. The bridge is much wider at each end than the midle and
was built at the cost of the publick for the benefitt of travelers."

many of the upper waters and smaller streams in the South.

In the early days riding on horseback was the chief mode of traveling on land, but in the seventeenth century wheeled vehicles appeared in Virginia and to a limited extent in the North, though for the purpose of carting rather than for driving. Hadley in Massachusetts had only five chaises in the town before 1795.[1] The usual styles were the two-wheeled and four-wheeled chaises with or without tops, the riding chair, sulky, and solo chair, which were little more than chaise bodies without tops, the curricle, phaeton, gig, calash, coach, and chariot. Sedan chairs could be hired by the hour in Charleston, and stagecoaches were in use in all the colonies. Four-wheeled chaises drawn by two horses could be transformed into one-horse chairs by taking off the front wheels, but coaches and chariots were generally drawn by four, six, and even eight horses. Chaises, curricles, and phaetons were the rule in the North, and coaches and chariots in Virginia and South Carolina; yet chairs and chaises were common enough in the South, and

[1] Hempstead, though mentioning a few chaises and chairs in New London, makes it clear in his diary that he never rode in one himself. He traveled always on horseback.

Henry Vassall of Massachusetts had his coach and chariot as well as his chaise and curricle. Many of the coaches and chariots were very ornate, neatly carved, handsomely gilded, lined with dove-colored, blue, and crimson cloth, and sometimes furnished with large front glass plates in one piece, with the arms of the owner on the door panels. The harness was bright with brass or silver-gilt metal work and ornamented with bells and finery, and coach and horses were adorned with plumes. Equipages of such magnificence appeared in Virginia as early as the first quarter of the eighteenth century. Chaises were more somber, though occasionally set off to advantage with brass hubs and wheel boxes. Though vehicles and harness were at first usually imported from England, chaise making in the North gradually developed into an industry, and chairs, chaises, and phaetons were frequently exported to Southern ports. Beverley once wrote to England for a set of secondhand harness from the royal mews, under the impression that some of them were very little the worse for wear, but when the consignment arrived he was greatly disappointed to discover that the harness was "sad trash not worth anything." In the Middle and New England colonies people usually traveled in winter in sleighs. These vehicles are described by Birket as standing "upon two pieces of wood that lyes flat on the ground like a North of England sled, the fore-part turning up with a bent to slyde over stones or any little rising and shod with smooth plates of iron to prevent their wearing away too fast."

We have now described in somewhat cursory fashion the leading characteristics and contrasts of colonial life in the eighteenth century. The description is manifestly not complete, for many interesting phases of that life have been left out of account. Little or nothing has been said of trade and business, money, newspapers, the postal serv-ice, prose and poetry, wit and humor, and the lighter side of government, politics, and the pro-fessions. To have made the account complete, something of each of these aspects of colonial life should have been included; but there are limita-tions of space and of material. Extensive as is the evidence available regarding the weightier aspects of early American life, there is but a slender resi-due from the vicissitudes of history to throw any sufficient light upon some of the habits, practices, and daily concerns of the colonists in the ordinary routine of their existence. Our forefathers on this continent were not given to talking about themselves, to gossiping on paper and in print, however much they may have gossiped in their daily intercourse, and to recording for future generations everyday matters that must have seemed to them trivial and commonplace. They have left us only a few letters of an intimate character, few diaries that are more than meager chronicles, and scarcely any picturesque anecdotes or narrations that have illustrative value in an attempt to reconstruct the daily life of the colonist.

Perhaps the greatest omission of all in a book of this character is the failure to speak of mental attitudes and opinions. What did the colonists think of each other, of the mother country, and of the foreign world that lay almost beyond their ken? One may readily discover contrasts in government, commerce, industry, agriculture, habits of life, and social relations, but it is not so easy for us nowadays to penetrate the colonist's mind, to fathom his motives, and to determine his likes and dislikes, fears and prejudices, jealousies and rivalries. In matters of opinion the colonists, except in New England, were not accustomed to disclose their inner thoughts, though it is not at all unlikely that large numbers of them had no inner thoughts to disclose. Moreover the people were of many origins, many minds, many varieties of temper, and grades of mental activity, and, as was to be expected, they differed very widely in their ideas on religion, conduct, and morals. They were Puritans, Quakers, and Anglicans; they were English, French, Germans, and Scots; and they were dwellers in seaports and inland towns, on small farms and large plantations, in the tidewater, in the upcountry, along the frontier, under temperate or semitropical skies.

As a consequence it is not to be wondered at that to the New Englander the well-known hospitality, good breeding, and politeness of the Southerners seemed little more than a sham in the face of their inhumanity and barbarity towards servants and slaves, their looseness of morals, and their fondness for horse racing, drinking, and gambling. Even Quincy himself, no ill-natured critic, could find in Virginia no courteous gentlemen and generous hosts but only "knaves and sharpers" given to practices that were "knavish and trickish." Fithian was warned that when he went to Virginia he would go "into the midst of many dangerous temptations; gay company, frequent entertainment, little practical devotion, no remote pretention to heart religion, daily examples in men of the highest quality of luxury, intemperence, and impiety."

Little more exact, on the other hand, was the Southerner's opinion of New England, to him a land of pretended holiness and disagreeable self-righteousness. He doubted the willingness of the New Englander to carry out his promises or to live up to his resolves; he dubbed him a saint, criticized his Yankee shrewdness, and charged him with business methods that were little short of thievery. These sentiments were not confined, however, to the people of the South. The Quakers also had a deep-seated antipathy for New England, in part because they remembered with bitterness and reproach the old-time treatment of their forerunners there. Stephen Collins of Philadelphia once called the merchants of Boston "deceitful, canting, Presbyterian deacons." Beekman of New York voiced a widespread feeling when he charged the men of Connecticut with selling goods under-weight, "a cursed fraud," and added that "seven-eights of the people I have credited in New England has proved to me [such] d—d ungreatful cheating fellows that I am now almost afraid to trust any man in Connecticut though he be well recommended from others." Often the lack in the North of open-handed hospitality and a polite demeanor toward strangers called forth remark. One traveler wrote that "the hospitality of the gentlemen of Carolina to strangers is a thing not known in our more northern region"; and John London of Wilmington said of New Haven, where he lived for some time, that "in general the manners of this place has more of bluntness than refinement and want those little attentions that constitute real politeness and are so agreeable to strangers." Such criticism was not unknown from New Englanders themselves, for Dr. Johnson once said that Punderson's failure as a clergyman was due to his "want of politeness," and Roger Wolcott named censoriousness, detraction, and drinking too much cider as the leading "blemishes" of Connecticut.

The fondness for innuendo and disparagement which these citations disclose was a characteristic colonial weakness. Virginians would speak of the ladies of Philadelphia as "homely, hard favored, and sour"; dwellers in Charleston would deem themselves vastly superior to their brethren of North Carolina; the old settlers of Boston, Philadelphia, and Charleston had little liking for the immigrant Germans and Scotch-Irish, were glad to get them out of the tidewater region into the country beyond, and looked upon them throughout the colonial period as inferior types of men, a "spurious race of mortals," as a Virginian called the Scotch-Irish.

Dislikes such as these cut deeply and found ample expression at all times, but were never more freely and harshly stated than in the years preceding the Revolution. The Stamp Act Congress, which was a gathering of a few high-minded men, was no real test of the situation. The Nonimportation Movement, as the first organized effort at common action against England on the part of the colonists as a whole and the first movement that really tested the temper of every grade and every section, made manifest, to a degree unknown before, the apparently hopeless disaccord that existed among the colonists everywhere on the eve of their combined revolt from the mother country. But this disagreement was more the inevitable accompaniment of the growth of national consciousness on the part of the American colonists than it was the manifestation of permanent and irreconcilable differences in their political, economic, and social life. To the early colonists must be given the credit of having laid a broad and stable foundation for the future United States of America, and their subsequent history has been the indisputable record of a growing national solidarity. Even the Civil War, which at first sight may seem conclusive contradiction, is to be regarded as in its essence the inevitable solution of hitherto discordant elements in the democracy which had their beginnings far back in the complex spiritual and social inheritance of the early colonial generations.

From the vantage point of the twentieth century, with its manifold legacy from the past and its ample promise for the future, it has been interesting to glance backward for a moment upon colonial times, to see once again the life of the people in all its energy, simplicity, and vivid coloring, with its crude and boisterous pleasures and its stern and uncompromising beliefs. Those forefathers of ours faced their gigantic tasks bravely and accomplished them sturdily, because they had within themselves the stuff of which a great nation is made. Differences among the colonists there indubitably were, but these, after all, were merely superficial distinctions of ancestral birth and training, beyond which shone the same common vision and the same broad and permanent ideals of free-dom, of life, opportunity, and worship. To the realization of these ideals the colonial folk dedi-cated themselves and so endured.

BIBLIOGRAPHICAL NOTE

THIS volume has been based in part upon memoranda of the writer drawn from contemporary manuscripts and newspapers and in part upon the following printed sources:

S. E. Sewall, *Diary*, 1679–1729, in the *Collections*, Mass. Hist. Soc., ser. v, vols. v–vii (1878–1882); *Journals of the Lives and Travels of Samuel Bownas and John Richardson* (1759); *Report of the Journey of Francis Louis Michel*, 1701–1702, *Va. Mag.*, vol. xxiv, (1916); T. Chalkley, *Journal*, 1703, Works (1790); *The Journals of Madam Knight and Rev. Mr. Buckingham* (Ed. Dwight, 1825); Esther Palmer and others, *Journal*, 1704–1705, Journal of Friends Hist. Soc., vi, 38–40, 63–71, 133–139; *Account of the Life and Travels of John Fothergill* (1753); T. Nairne, *Letter from South Carolina*, 1710 (2d ed., 1732); *A Brief Journal of the Life, Travels, and Labours of Love . . . of Thomas Wilson* (1784); J. Dickinson, *Journal*, 1714, Friends Library, xii; H. Jones, *Present State of Virginia*, 1724 (Sabin reprint, 1865); J. Hempstead, *Diary*, in the collections of the New London County Historical Society, i (1901); *Diary of a Voyage from Rotterdam to Philadelphia in 1728*, Pa. Germ. Soc. Publ., xviii; J. Brickell, *Natural History of North Carolina*, 1737 (1911); *Writings of Colonel William Byrd of Westover* (Bassett ed., 1901); S. Checkley, *Diary*,

1735, Publ. Col. Soc. Mass., XII, 270–306; R. Chapman,
Letters, 1739–1740, William and Mary Quarterly, XXI;
Abstract of the Journal of E. Peckover's Travels, 1742–
1743, Friends Hist. Soc., I, 95–109; J. McSparran, *A
Letter Book and Abstract of our Services*, 1743–1751
(1899); W. Logan, *Journal*, 1745, Pa. Mag., XXXVI,
1–16, 162–186; J. Emerson, *Diary*, 1748–1749, in
Proceedings, Mass. Hist. Soc., XLIV, 263–282; G. Fisher,
Narrative, 1750, William and Mary Quarterly, XVII, 147–
175; *Extracts from Capt. Goelet's Journal*, 1746–1750, New
England Hist. and Gen. Reg., XXIV, 50–63, reprinted,
with additions and notes by Albert H. Hoyt (1870);
J. Birket, *Some Cursory Remarks*, 1750–1751 (1916);
P. Kalm, *Travels into North America*, 1748–1751 (1772);
Diary of a Journey of the Moravians, 1753, in *Travels in
the American Colonies* (N. D. Mereness, ed., 1916); T.
Thompson, *An Account of Two Missionary Voyages*
(1758); A. Burnaby, *Travels* (Wilson ed., 1904); R.
Wolcott, *Memoir Relating to Connecticut, Collections*,
Conn. Hist. Soc., III, pp. 325–336; J. Boucher, *Letters*,
1759–1772, Md. Mag., VII; Lord A. Gordon, *Journal*,
1764–1765, in *Travels in the American Colonies* (1916);
*An Account of East Florida with a Journal, Kept by J.
Bartram* (1766); W. Eddis, *Letters*, 1769–1777 (1792);
P. Webster, *Journal*, 1765, *Publications*, Southern
History Association (1898); J. Quincy, Jr., *Southern
Journal*, 1773, *Proceedings*, Mass. Hist. Soc., vol. XLIX,
June, 1916; J. Harrower, *Diary*, 1773–1776, Amer. Hist.
Rev., October, 1900; P. Fithian, *Journal and Letters*,
1767–1774 (1900); J. D. Schoepf, *Travels in the Con-
federation*, 1783–1784 (1911); J. F. D. Smyth, *A Tour in
the United States* (1784); and various diaries in the *His-
torical Collections* of the Essex Institute. In addition

many scattered documents, letters, wills, inventories, invoices, commercial and legal records, printed in the publications of historical societies and elsewhere, have been used.

It is impossible to give here any adequate bibliography of the secondary works dealing with the various aspects of the subject. There is no single book which covers the whole field nor indeed any volume which treats fully the topics presented in any one of the chapters. On the other hand, there are many admirable books which present with great fulness of detail selected aspects of colonial life — houses, dress, manners, and customs — but usually with the intent of satisfying only the needs of the general reader. There are also excellent writings of a more technical and scholarly character dealing with racial elements, land, labor, and education, but, except Professor Jernegan in his forthcoming work on education in the colonies, no one, as far as I know, has made a sustained attempt to study these topics on a large scale with an eye to their historical significance. The histories of individual States are of very little value in this connection, and local histories, though indispensable to the student, are often restricted in scope and provincial in treatment. Some of the town and county histories are, however, excellent, but the list is too long to be given here.

Deserving of notice are F. B. Dexter, *Estimates of Population, Proceedings*, American Antiquarian Society (1887), reprinted in Dexter, *A Selection from the Miscellaneous Historical Papers of Fifty Years* (1918), pp. 153–178; L. J. Fosdick, *French Blood in America* (1906); C. K. Bolton, *Scotch Irish Pioneers* (1910); H. J. Ford, *The Scotch Irish in America* (1915); A. B. Faust, *The*

German Element in the United States (1909); L. F. Bittinger, *The Germans in Colonial Times* (1901); Amandus Johnson, *Swedish Elements on the Delaware* (1911); J. P. Maclean, *An Historical Account of the Settlements of Scotch Highlanders in America* (1900); C. P. Gould, *Land System* and *Money and Transportation in Maryland*, Johns Hopkins University Studies, XXXI, XXXIII, (1913, 1915); articles by Judge Smith on towns and baronies in South Carolina, in the *South Carolina Historical and Genealogical Magazine;* A. D. Mellick, *Story of an Old Farm* (1889); I. N. P. Stokes, *The Iconography of Manhattan Island* (1916); Mrs. M. M. P. (N.) Stanard, *Colonial Virginia, its People and Customs* (1917); and C. C. Jones, *Dead Towns of Georgia* (1878).

Among the best of the general books bearing on our subject are these: H. D. Eberlein, *The Architecture of Colonial America* (1915); H. D. Eberlein and A. McClure, *The Practical Book of Early American Arts and Crafts* (1916); H. D. Eberlein and H. M. Lippincott, *The Colonial Homes of Philadelphia and its Neighborhood* (1912); J. M. Hammond, *Colonial Mansions of Maryland and Delaware* (1914); W. J. Mills, *Historic Houses of New Jersey* (1902); Mrs. A. M. (L.) Sioussat, *Old Manors in the Colony of Maryland* (two parts, 1911, 1913); R. A. Lancaster, *Historic Virginia Homes and Churches* (1915); *Colonial Churches in the Original Colony of Virginia* (1908); A. R. H. Smith, *The Dwelling Houses of Charleston* (1917); H. M. Lippincott, *Early Philadelphia* (1917); Mrs. A. M. Earle, *Home Life in Colonial Days* (1898) and *Child Life in Colonial Days* (1899); Mrs. M. W. Goodwin, *The Colonial Cavalier* (1894); A. S. Huntington, *Under a Colonial Roof Tree* (1891); W. R. Bliss, *Colonial Times* on *Buzzards Bay* (1889); J. B. Felt, *Customs of New England* (1853); C. S. Phelps, *Rural Life in Litchfield County* (1917); P. W. Bidwell, *Rural Economy in New England* (1916; though dealing with the period after 1800, this work is very suggestive for the eighteenth century); F. H. Bigelow, *Historic Silver of the Colonies and its Makers* (1917); E. McClellan, *Historic Dress in America* (1910); A. W. Calhoun, *A Social History of the American Family* (1917); R. M. Tryon, *Household Manufactures* (1917); E. Field, *The Colonial Tavern* (1897); G. O. Seilhamer, *History of the American Theater* (1891); F. S. Child, *The Colonial Parson* and *A Colonial Parish* (1896, 1911); A. E. Bostwick, *The American Public Library* (1910); W. L. Hubbard, *The American History and Encyclopædia of Music* (1908–10) 12 v.; L. C. Elson, *History of American Music* (rev. ed., 1915); S. Dunbar, *A History of Travel in America* (1915); and G. R. Putnam, *Lighthouses and Lightships* (1917). A model study of its kind, for our purpose, is S. F. Batchelder, *Notes on Colonel Henry Vassall, Publications,* Cambridge Hist. Soc., x, 5–85.

Columbia University in its Contributions to Education, Teachers College Series, has issued a number of valuable monographs on phases of colonial education and apprenticeship. Elsewhere may be found books and monographs on negro and Indian slavery and white servitude, designed rather for the scholar than the general reader. Nothing of importance has been written on the convict system.

INDEX